For Franklin and Marshall College
with best greetings

John Rowe Workman

2/28/59.

NEW HORIZONS OF
HIGHER EDUCATION

NEW HORIZONS OF HIGHER EDUCATION

Innovation and Experimentation at Brown University

By JOHN ROWE WORKMAN

Associate Professor of Classics, Brown University

INTRODUCTION BY JOHN W. GARDNER, PRESIDENT, CARNEGIE CORPORATION

Public Affairs Press, Washington, D. C.

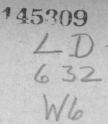
ABOUT THE AUTHOR

Dr. John Rowe Workman has been on the faculty of Brown University since 1947. He has taught in both the experimental and standard curriculum.

Born in Lancaster, Pennsylvania, in 1918, he took his bachelor's and doctor's degrees in Classics at Princeton. In 1952-53 he held an internship in General Education to teach Humanities at Columbia College in New York. During 1953-54 he was engaged in research in Roman Law and Greek Philosophy at the University of Edinburgh, Scotland.

He is the author of a number of translations from Greek and Latin, and numerous articles in encyclopedias.

At Brown where he is now associate professor of Classics, Dr. Workman has been Assistant to the Dean of the College and a member of the Board of Counselors.

INTRODUCTION

In conducting a symphony some years ago, Toscanini is said to have observed that the new second violinist maintained throughout the performance an expression of acute pain. Toscanini sought him out later and asked whether he were ill. The answer was "No." Angry? "No." Trouble in the family? "No." Then what was wrong? The violinist grimaced and said, "I hate music!"

Some college presidents, deans and professors would give the same response with respect to teaching if the penalties for such candor were not so high.

Brown University has had the very good fortune to have presidents, deans and professors who care a great deal about teaching. The students at Brown cannot be expected to know how lucky they are.

Almost any first-rate college teacher can draw up a significant list of broad educational goals that should govern the early years of college before the student has begun to specialize. And when various people draw up such lists, they exhibit a fair measure of agreement. The great difficulty is to create the educational situations in which such goals may be attained.

Important innovations in college teaching can only be accomplished by men with a thorough mastery of subject matter and an imaginative grasp of the teaching process. Beyond that they need time, energy, and courage. Any substantial innovation in the curriculum disturbs comfortable habits and threatens vested interests on the faculty. Only a faculty which is intellectually vigorous will attempt such an innovation. And only a faculty which is largeminded and courageous will carry it through.

Brown University has accomplished such an innovation in the program described by Professor Workman. I have talked with students who have participated in this experiment, and I have no doubt of its impact on them. Students are usually grateful for an educational experience which brings them to life intellectually and lures them into active coping with ideas.

Unfortunately, successful teaching is not an easily visible thing. Successful teaching might stand out more starkly if ineffective teaching could be properly appraised. If there were some way to demonstrate how many thousands of students on a given campus on a week-day morning simply were *not* listening to the lecture; if it were possible to count the tens of thousands of students over the country who are getting literally nothing out of page after page of reading assignments; if it were possible to make visible the inertness, the apathy, the empti-ness of much that passes for education—memorizing trivial facts, filing away the instructor's pet opinions, learning to judge shrewdly what will be asked on examinations—if all of these depressing truths could be demonstrated, then the vital successes in education would ring triumphantly in the college halls.

How applicable is the Brown experiment to other institutions? That is not an easy question to answer. I believe that every college profes-sor seriously interested in undergraduate liberal education should read this book. But I have never been impressed with the possibility that one could develop at one institution a "formula" for liberal education which could be copied by all others. Accomplishing good under-graduate liberal education is a highly creative task. A college faculty which has achieved this has created something that cannot be copied—something blended of their own experience and talents, the character and background of their students, and the resources of their institution.

And yet this book will have many lessons for anyone launching a similar enterprise. Certainly college teachers everywhere might pro-fitably emulate the intellectual vigor and flexibility, the devotion to teaching and the high seriousness of the group which accomplished this important work at Brown.

JOHN W. GARDNER

President, The Carnegie Corporation of New York

CONTENTS

ACKNOWLEDGMENTS

The writer freely acknowledges his primary sources: the addresses of Presidents Wriston and Keeney, conversations with the Secretary of the Faculty and of the Committee on the Curriculum, Professor Herbert N. Couch, and five groups of Brunonians and Pembrokers who have probed the mysteries of Vergil's MAIVS OPVS as the "rising Generation." He is grateful also to Mrs. Dorothea Borden for a masterful job in transcribing the text.

JOHN ROWE WORKMAN

Providence, Rhode Island

I Roots of Experiment

"The true test of civilization is not the census, nor the size of cities, nor the crops—no, but the kind of man the country turns out."

—RALPH WALDO EMERSON.

The search for the ideal curriculum in school and college is a continuing process. There are moments when it would seem to be the exclusive trust of academicians as discussion about experimentation or change becomes a topic at lunch in the faculty club, this especially after an exhausting morning devoted to teaching the nature of bucolic poetry to undergraduates who are anticipating the vernal advent of Venus and Bacchus during the annual spring weekend. It may become an afterglow in the professorial mind after the results of the senior comprehensives have been computed and the bluebooks filed away among departmental records.

At other times the curriculum becomes the concern of the body politic, and war or national emergency or some peculiar or alarming social condition stimulates a sudden interest in what is being taught and how this is being conveyed. The educational sociologist might even demonstrate that a curriculum is affected by war. Within our own generation there is ample evidence that the first World War brought about a disintegration of the venerable classical curriculum. World War II introduced a pattern of thinking about the goals and objectives of liberal education which has asserted itself in the restoration of some of the aspects of philosophical content which characterized the liberal arts through the Middle Ages, the Renaissance, and the Age of Enlightenment. The thinking behind these curricular reforms may have been governed by extensive traveling and by communication with other educational systems and the products of these during World War II. Certainly any American who experiences foreign education must admit that the American fondness for mechanism and administration and other paraphernalia of technique is inalienably associated with teaching and education and the academic curriculum at all levels.

Again, in a time of national emergency we are witnessing another hue and cry about education. Once more there will be a change, a "re-emphasis" as the officials term it. The commonwealth is calling for it; its desirability is proclaimed from pulpit and editorial page and the halls of Congress. Mathematicians and Latinists are hopeful; physicists and chemists are taking to their storm-cellars. The outcome will likely be another readjustment, a new shifting of emphases, or, as one sardonic educationalist has put it, "another inquest into the hot and cold running regulations."

In all of this concern about a curriculum and about educational goals it is a curious but documented fact that the most silent group is the alumni of our colleges and universities of liberal arts. While these folk frequently demonstrate a lively interest in communal responsibilities by serving on school boards or by making contributions to the increasingly popular alumni funds of annual giving at their colleges, their abiding concern with education is not very incisive. Whether they have come to regard this as the concern of the faculty alone, whether they have reached an abortive conclusion that there is a line of separation between the academic mind and the practice of the marketplace, whether they have failed to gain an insight during their collegiate days that education and the curriculum are a vital and growing entity that does not end when they are graduated, we are not in a position to say. We are suspicious, however, that previous curricula have failed to motivate the whole man. This lack of motivation is the by-product of generations of mistaken emphasis in educational ideals. The student in grade school learns his multiplication tables by rote; the college student all too frequently continues to memorize and to acquire information by rote. It is all very well for him to study Greek tragedy or the principles of mathematical logic or the nature of American government; unless he can bring to these his own experience and his own powers of reasoning he will spend four years in college and, probably the rest of his life, in a mechanical process of memorizing facts and classifying data without even so much as a challenge or a source of motivation beyond a degree and a respectable position. He may well aspire to a position of eminence in his profession or vocation but sooner or later he will yearn for a scissors to extricate himself from the web which he himself has been spinning.

The curriculum of Brown University has undergone many changes since the institution was chartered in 1764. In each search for a curriculum the philosophy of education has been assessed and examined—not for the first time at the end of World Wars I and II. The names of Manning and Wayland and Andrews are symbolic of curricular concern since the days of the University's foundation; they signify, in each instance, something of an educational revolution, and the impact of their reforms has transcended the Providence Plantations and the United States. Nor is there any reason to believe that these names will stand alone in the impact of Brown upon American higher education. The Charter of the University presents the challenge when it speaks about the aims of a liberal education: "by forming the rising Generation to Virtue Knowledge & useful Literature & thus preserving in the Community a Succession of Men duly qualify'd for discharging the Offices of Life with usefulness and reputation . . . ." The spirit of the Charter, then, makes bold the idea of experimentation; examination of the past tradition corroborates this, underscoring the motivation of the "rising Generation" and a perspicacious concern for its future. Curricular revision without examination of educational goals and a projection into the means and purpose of a liberal education intimates an academic side show without a main performance. Too frequently a curriculum is revised either to satisfy the whims or the prejudices of pressure groups within a faculty or else to conform with a fetish which can be emulated but not successfully integrated; this fetish may have its origin in other universities or colleges but it is more likely to arise in the marketplace among those least likely to be perceptive of the nature of the liberal arts.

These chapters seek to clarify the thinking which led to the experimental curriculum, known as the Identification and Criticism of Ideas, at Brown. They are highly subjective as they explore the operation of the academic mind and the nettles of danger which all education presents. More pertinently they represent several of the problems which must be considered in the formulation of any curriculum, secondary or collegiate, problems of challenge, problems of any philosophy of education.

On the evening of February 29, 1952, President Henry M. Wriston proposed an experimental form of education before the departmental chairmen of Brown University. For the origin of this proposal, history moves back to the dark days of World War II, to the year 1943, when this concept was devised by Bruce M. Bigelow, late professor of history at Brown and vice-president of the University. Between his idealistic projection of these courses and the translation of the proposal's essence into the program of the Identification and Criticism of Ideas there was much work involving many people and still more ideas. Yet the element of the ideal persevered and it has permeated the fabric of the whole University as a lively testament of Bigelow's own vitality and the unique originality of his idea. Among students these courses are known popularly as "The IC Program;" among members of the administration and the Committee on the Curriculum they are frequently referred to as "the experimental program."

A spectrum-analysis of the concept of education upon which courses in this program are predicated would reveal many hues of intellectual and administrative complexity: motivation of students, development of clear thinking, enhanced powers of articulation, sensitive incorporation of experience into the realization of attained knowledge, communication with the creative processes by which great thinkers and artists have made their contributions to thought and society, affirmation that the process of education is as vital after graduation as it is the first two years of college. There are many other aspects and and implications and demands. Moreover, two immediate and mundane prerequisites had to be satisfied: the courses had to have some relevance to the education which the lowerclassmen experienced in school and which they presented for admission to Brown and Pembroke; also the proposed courses had to be, in some measure, propaedeutic to upper-class concentration within an area or field of scholarship.

As the experiment began in the academic year 1953-54 the several departments were invited to present courses. In each course a central classic or two was submitted, at departmental or the professor's choice, for a year's intensive study of the ideas which it might contain. Frequently the classic selected for analysis and examination was that work which represented an original landmark of creative thinking within a field—Darwin's *Origin of Species* in Biology, Adam Smith's *Wealth of Nations* in Economics, Plato's *Republic* in Philosophy. To isolate and criticize the inherent ideas was the challenge to the student; to moderate the discussion and to draw up the specifications of the course became the role for the professor; to enhance communication and discussion the number of students in each class was limited to twenty; to ensure some modicum of success at the outset of the experiment students were selected who ranked in the upper half of their class, freshmen on the basis of their records at school and in the College Boards, sophomores upon their record at Brown during freshman year. While there was a flurry of excitement in the launching of the new courses, manifesting itself in such accidentals as a rather dramatic drop, on Wall Street, of the stocks of several publishing houses the day it was announced that Brown was abolishing textbooks and was going classical, or, again, in the failure of the computing machines in the Recorder's office to carry the initials I.C.I. in designation of the new courses—hence IC, for the machine will carry only two letters—or in some difficulty with U.S. Customs to have some copies of a treatise on Marxism published in Russia cleared for use in a course in Political Science—while such incidentals underscore the dramatic moments of the program's launching, it was the willingness of the Faculty of Brown University to examine and to activate the principles of President Wriston's proposal and the generous grant from the Carnegie Corporation to assist in meeting increased instructional expenses which enabled the first courses to be presented. For the Faculty it was an act both of faith and of initiative, faith in the merit of the idea and in the future of the University, initiative to rise to an experiment for the "rising Generation." For the Carnegie Corporation it was a sizable investment in its perpetual concern with instruction and advancement of learning.

Under the leadership of President Barnaby C. Keeney the experimental atmosphere has continued and the program expanded. While the experimental courses have been merged with the standard curriculum by a vote of the Faculty on February 4, 1958, there is no indication that curricular interest and the spirit of quest for maintaining the perfect curriculum have abated or will terminate. That President Keeney was Dean of the College when the experimental program was initiated and is himself the chairman of the Committee on the Curriculum ensures the enlightened concern of the administration for what is taught and how it is taught, the strongest foundation for education in the liberal arts. That new courses in the IC program are added every year, while original IC courses are constantly being examined and renewed, is the best testimonial to the enthusiasm of professor and student alike for the program.

II Goals and the Classics

> ". . . . our argument shows that there is a resident faculty in the soul
> of every person, and an instrument enabling each of us to learn; and
> so this faculty or instrument must be turned away from the perishing
> world until it can endure to contemplate the real world and its brightest
> part which is the Idea . . . ." — PLATO

The last two years of secondary school and the first two of college
constitute a very formative period in a student's educational experience. In the last two years of school the student suddenly finds
himself confronted with problems which can affect the rest of his
life. Freshman and sophomore years at college see him making
choices that will determine his vocation or profession, his tastes, his
social relations. One or two choices may even indicate whether he
will be able to enter his junior year.

These four years present a set of challenges. One significant challenge of which the student will become increasingly aware is the
matter of choosing a college. This entails even deeper consideration:
what institution will accommodate him, for it is only after deep reflection, considerable correspondence, and the dispatch of numerous
application fees that the student will begin to examine himself and
ask whether he has the qualifications to enter college. Once admitted,
only a few of the more enlightened students will ask, in all earnest-
ness, what course they will pursue.

In a sense the student is carried along to his conclusions by the
nature of his environment. Parental pressure may dictate the choice
of college; it may even specify the course he is to follow, though in
the latter respect parents are an obstacle to young people and a
genuine nuisance, however indirectly, to admissions officers and deans
and professors in their insistence upon the type of collegiate work
their offspring must study. Almost as profound an influence is exercised by the student's contemporaries. A modern college's office
of public relations may communicate the achievements of former
acquaintances now in college. Admissions officers spread sunshine
and sweetness in their annual visits to the school. Reports from
returning alumni whet the prospective undergraduate's appetite for
the freedom and independence which are said to signify life in college.

In many schools students are quick to discern the mark of sophistication associated with having to take the "College Boards." So far as the college or university is concerned, the most that it can hope to realize for itself in this process is a reputation as a place where, in addition to athletics and freedom (for thus nonsense is frequently construed in the popular mind), courses are offered which will enable the student to make money upon graduation. Occasionally this reputation undergoes qualification, and the institution is conceived to be a filling station where preparation is made for medical school or engineering school or some other practically useful activity like that. It is no wonder that professors teaching freshmen and the deans who counsel them wince when these neophytes reveal the parental and popular understanding of higher education. As for the liberal arts, their martyrdom has always been a protracted and precarious existence.

In college, the student is faced with another set of problems, though the conditions of influence differ from those in secondary schools. Through the haze frequently generated by complex curricula, extracurricular activities, and adjustment to the freedom of academic life, the student perceives that it will be necessary for him to select courses and to choose a field of concentration for his upperclass years. Here again there is a challenge, and the student must decide whether future economic considerations or his own personal inclinations will determine his major study of junior and senior years. Happily neither proves a criterion at times. Moreover, should he prepare himself for graduate school, or should he try to get a liberal education for life? What stock should he put in academic fads, in cross-departmental areas of concentration, in fields which he never heard of until he took the introductory course during freshman year?

These four years, then, interrupted only by a burst of oratory at commencement in preparatory school or of academic ceremony as his freshman year opens, are an integral unit in the student's education. If, as Aristotle asserts, character is determined by choice, then the character of the student is surely formed in the midst of guidance directors, faculty counselors, parents, deans, and all sorts and conditions of experts who have gotten into the act during these four years. Upon graduation from school the student is exhorted variously to be an individualist, to fight for what is identified as the right, to remain aloof from the perils of life . . . . the stock themes of those whose specialty is to arouse young minds with platitudes.

Once in college the same student is told that not all is well in the world, that the truth alone will make him free, that he must avoid complacency and the Protean aspect of security, and that his college career will be exactly what he makes of it. All of this, within a short period of four months, served up with freshman IQ tests and the light refreshments of some fifty teas and receptions during freshman orientation, makes for a good case of indigestion or, on occasion, business for the college psychiatrist. The problem here would seem to be one of transition. Yet the problem is one also of translation, translation of all this advice, translation of the student's background and conditioning into a specific course of study. What is frequently overlooked, however, is that the academic highway is strewn with the living corpses of engineers turned humanists, of pre-medicals who, failing to meet the requirements in chemistry, have settled for a concentration in biology with the hope that they will sell themselves to a pharmaceutical firm upon graduation; some few of them may become historians or sociologists; there is always room in life for an English major.

The exercise of choice and the meeting of a challenge, however, no matter how skillfully motivated and handled, have a habit of uncovering certain weaknesses in institutions and in character. A challenge may be met with a blaze of bravado or a gale of glory. That it should be is a tribute to the daring enthusiasm of youth. Less is said about the inadequacies that come to light after choice has been exercised. It is difficult to place the blame on the students when, in reality, they are victims of a system which sanctions these weaknesses.

One weakness, perhaps the most striking, has been the needless repetition of courses in the last two years in high school and the underclass years at college. Here there is a waste of time and energy that can infect the very moral fiber of the student. It can end any degree of motivation. Again the same problem which gets so much attention from parents, PTA's, and school boards, the problem of promotion in the elementary grades is equally cogent at the secondary level; obviously the same freshman course which accommodates the bright student from a mediocre school may not be the fare for the slow student who has attended a preparatory school of impressive vintage. Yet the conventional freshman course can easily serve to perpetuate this disparity, accenting it to a point of no return in unity of either life or learning in college. Such a course will begin as a vehicle of wisdom and enlightenment, but it will soon develop into a bromide of social and scholastic adjustment, as the slow student is dragged along by the able student until the latter loses his interest for lack of inspiration.

Here certainly there is desirability of some challenge. It does not take a Plato to prove that the barnacles of indifference and sloth soon affix themselves to a nature that has no sense of direction, a mind not exhorted to new pursuits and new interests. The records of freshmen who entered college well prepared but who have collapsed in the first term amply attest this.

Again, in spite of the good intentions of guidance counselors in school and faculty advisers in college, the student in his lust for academic diversion will hop and skip from subject to subject, never learning anything thoroughly but accumulating a patchwork of subjects pursued but never mastered. In some institutions it becomes a pall of semester hours, impressive as they are mustered on the graduating certificate, but representing virtually nothing in the way of an education—interment rather than initiation. This must not be considered a criticism of education in breadth; it is rather a reflection upon the pressures which descend upon the student as he seeks to interpret curricular requirements, hints from his parents, the counsel of advisers, and tips from his contemporaries. This weakness is even more glaring as the student possesses high natural endowments.

Finally there is the matter of maturity, of growing up in the image of a liberal education. A curriculum can assist the student here, the devoted teacher can add to his stature, but in the final analysis it is up to the student's own initiative to determine what he is, to define his goals in life, and then to establish his method of procedure in realizing his ideal. Unless the student is made aware of his existence, his religious and social obligations, and the sheer fact that he is a human being living in this world, he cannot be expected to define any significant purpose in his life or to derive anything useful from education.

So far as the college is concerned, the most significant facet of a freshman or sophomore course is its virtue as a vehicle in the process of maturing the natural man. Many elements can contribute to this process. Not least is the idea of a residential college, well summarized by Henry Merritt Wriston in his "emphasis upon dormitories as instruments of instruction" and in his conviction that a community of scholarship will promote the very ends of a liberal education. There are many who believe that a coffee lounge in the building for student activities can be as productive of creative ideas as the graduate seminary rooms in the library. Athletics, on the collegiate level, likewise can assist in the process of adjustment toward maturity; in the American system we are fortunate that so much emphasis has been put on sports in spite of all the fussiness these involve. This is a common bond among students in school; at college it is more cosmopolitan in its outlook, and the program has attained a degree of variety which can more effectively meet the interests, participative or for spectacle, of a greater number of students than the football-baseball-basketball triumvirate in most secondary schools. Then there are extra-curricular activities in journalism, drama, political expression—to mention a few—which leave varying degrees of impression upon students. Participation in these will enhance the maturing process and academic adjustment.

But the fact still remains, it is pre-eminently the expression of the classroom that potentially converts the young man and the young woman from a creature possessed of opinions and odd facts of information to a human being capable of forming valid judgments and sensitive to the pertinent responses of reason and the emotions. Thus a student who enters college with the unrecognized fact but very real hardship of a great many prejudices and exaggerated ideas about himself and other members of society will be less insecure and will develop a dimension of mental objectivity, once he has been exposed to a chapter or two of the history of humanity. Conversely, the young person who has a penchant for generalization, to whom vagueness has become a fine art as a result of an illusive life at home or at school, can profit from an examination of primary source material and, in turn, should attain to a more precise regard for the law and the letter thereof.

It must remain a pious hope that undergraduate institutions will ameliorate both conditions of weakness. Frequently but not always so salutarily the lecturer in a lowerclass course can achieve the desired effect in each instance. But here there is the drawback; the student without objectivity may retreat farther into his shell of satisfying prejudice; he will become even more determined in his opinions, for there is no challenge; rhetoric can lull as well as evoke responses. Physically, at least, the latter is virtually impossible, as the atmosphere of a lecture hall is not conducive to the airing of opinions. Similarly the student who generalizes can hardly be expected to cultivate a spirit of differentiation when he hears his lecturer "boil down" whole eras of culture and ages of accomplishment into 50 minutes of polished edification. And so it is rather the Socratic method of discussion, of analysis and dialectic between teacher and student and between students, that we aver to be the most effective form of education in the development of the mature man.

In the upperclass years, from time to time, we meet a student who is able to elude our prescription for adjustment and maturity, and these few exceptions, sometimes stigmatized as "campus lawyers," are those who were successful in beating the system, who have literally short-circuited their own development. These become, in turn, the hounds who seek "cold dope" for senior comprehensives; these are the characters who will be bent into shape by the iron judgment of the world whether it be a master sergent in the army or a foreman of a plant or public opinion. The sooner the student is presented with a challenge, with something that will make him think, the sooner he will grow up.

It should be stated, however, that the spirit of challenge may be most poignantly underscored if its essence evokes a response from the student's own experience. In the subject of history of art, for instance, though it may pertain to philosophy or psychology just as effectively, one way to arouse a student's own response comes in the question whether the student places a higher value on a photograph than on an oil painting of his girl. That some difference pertains between these two media probably has never occurred to him; yet his sentiments are likely to be strong in this matter and indeed immediate. Not only is he faced with making a choice, but more particularly a significant ingredient in his choice is a personal one, conditioned by his own emotions and by something that has occurred within his own experience.

Most of the early years of school are spent in experiencing what might be called the atmosphere of public opinion. This experience assumes many forms and degrees of intensity. It begins when a child realizes that there are other people in the world beside himself. Techniques of discipline have at their root comparison of people or the atmosphere of opinion. It is a sanction which seems to be universal. Praise or censure from teachers is as strong as it is from contemporaries. Now this very atmosphere of public opinion is a decisive factor in education; rightly or wrongly it is perhaps the most active agent in the process of maturity. In its extreme form it is ridicule or even physical violence. But in assaults from classmates upon a student's beliefs we see the most effective means of bestirring his own thoughts, of arousing his convictions and, incidentally, his knowledge in support of his conclusions. The bar of public opinion is strong and it can be vicious. In the lowerclass years, however, it is extremely vital, for it moves the student to be articulate, to measure and to refine his argument in the light of the best evidence he can muster. Without the reasoned moderation of a teacher who knows the ramifications of the subject and without the impetuosity of contemporaries whose experience is similar, though not identical with the student's, it is unlikely that much will be gained in the adjustment that is vital in the first two years of college.

But there is another aspect of lowerclass instruction at college and one upon which more certain evaluation may be placed than the rather immeasurable quality of maturity. A college is concerned with an adequate basis of knowledge upon which a subsequent plan of concentration can be built. The question may well be raised about the relation of lowerclass courses to more advanced and more specialized topics in the academic field or area.

In former days the American colonial college held fast to the semblance of medieval education with emphasis upon depth of learning within four or five fields. Here was a solidarity of training that admitted little room for personal whims; imposed from above, it stood the test of many generations as the qualifications of an educated man. In addition to the linguistic and rhetorical training that came with the Greek and Latin classics, these provided a useful and an ornamental discipline in moral values and in scientific reckoning. But social and economic forces were to change all that. The implications of the Industrial Revolution, the expansion of educational opportunity, the rise of vocational training, and the intensification of the traditional disciplines through increased scientific investigation—each is reflected in the modern curriculum. For instance, it has been traditional to observe psychological motifs in the tragic characters of Euripides; the Romans were aware of this, and it became the source of motivation and interest in their own tragedies. The Renaissance capitalized upon it as the rebirth of European letters sought to employ a new realism in portrayal of character. As a science, however, psychology did not develop until the 20th century; its rise can be attributed in part to the emergence of biology from the medieval domination of Aristotelian science. But what of Euripides? The same technique of research which liberated biology and originated psychology began to evaporate all humanistic values from this Greek tragedian, and in place of the liberal interpretation of the Euripidean message scholars became content to count the number of times prepositions or particles occur.

A movement initiated by a President of Brown in the 19th century, Francis Wayland, pointed to the eventual demise of the traditional pattern of education. As a panacea for the pressures which threatened the old classical system, Wayland actually proposed a form of universal education. In this process he forecast a system of free-course election in which each student assumed the responsibility for his educational pattern. This soon released a tidal wave of new subjects beyond the established disciplines and, while Wayland's fundamental idea, *viz.* that a student must participate in the concern for his own educational progress, while this idea was both good and revolutionary, it required little imagination to see that any fiber of discipline would soon disappear as students pursued courses to their own fancy, effecting a patchwork of credits neither liberal nor educational. Courses were elected because of the oratorical powers of the lecturers; others came within the shadow of vocational implications, and the economics of a livelihood dictated some choices; the absence of an hour test or a term paper determined the popularity of many a course; vagaries of personal choice governed many of the elections. Wayland's proposal, therefore, became a panacea not so much to meet the problems of the smaller college of liberal arts; it was adopted and adapted on a large scale as academic policy while America expanded physically and ideologically.

This pattern prevailed until the end of World War II. Our colleges unleashed upon society graduates who had presumably acquired a liberal education in terms which the students themselves had dictated. Save for some semblance of a major subject pursued in junior and senior years, the bachelor's degree represented a melange of subjects chosen without any particular philosophy of education. To effect some synthesizing force, what many educationalists term "integration," i.e. to introduce both depth and breadth in an assortment of courses, post-war curricula sought again to arouse in the student some concern for his education; but they also pointed out some responsibility and discipline that the defined ends of education might be fulfilled. Here our second aspect assumes pertinence. In the wilderness of requirements and prerequisites, a curriculum must be aware of the steps in preparing students for upperclass concentration. In the midst of experimentation, of providing the student with a knowledge of several areas and disciplines, and of seeking educational breadth, it is well to ask what sense of unity does a curriculum provide that the student will possess all the intangible values of which deans and college presidents speak. Can these ends be met at the same time that the faculty is satisfied, for the main interest of a professor is depth of scholarship within a field?

Various answers have been sought in the survey course, in the distribution course, in the topical course. Each has virtue, each has limitations. The survey course sacrifices technique of method and discipline within a field or area for chronological comprehensiveness. Historical framework is fully preserved in the survey course, but the systematic side suffers. Superficiality is encouraged by the treatment of names, dates, trends, and other phenomens associated with the subject in question. Implications, inherent relationships, and examples of systematic thinking yield, in a survey course, to the parade of facts and movements; these react upon the student in such a way as to give him the impression that all of man's experience, in whatever dimension expressed, can be reduced to a skeleton or synopsis. This is the level of the Five-Foot Shelf, of the *Reader's Digest,* and of other Chautauquan techniques that seek to edify society by desensitizing the history of man's experience and achievement and by serving it up already digested. Within recent years one university has gone so far as to publish an encyclopedia of ideas—a survey for those who lack spontaneity of impulse to seek out ideas for themselves, let alone weigh the validity of an idea. But the fact remains, with the survey course, that, while it may contribute an adequate historical panorama of events and trends, it does not increase the student's understanding of scholarly techniques, of research, and of the application of the mind to a body of data. The evils of secondary-school memorization of facts, as well as a stagnating effect so far as upper-class collegiate concentration goes, mark the survey course, in our estimation, as no inherent academic discipline at all.

The distribution course is a phenomenon of the curricular revisions that came at the end of World War II. Unlike the survey course the course in distribution has, as its end, discipline in the manner of thinking in a particular subject or field. It represents depth of investigation rather than breadth. The purpose is to acquaint students with a pertinent field, the avenues of approach, and the method of initiating investigation and seeking solutions for problems within that field. The body of material in a distribution course ranges from basic elements to problems of scholarship. Now the distribution course satisfies two most important needs of the freshman curriculum, *viz.* the diffusion of knowledge and a cogent form of mental activity. It is open to censure on occasions, and here the spoils system of faculty seniority comes to the fore. Too frequently the former survey course has been revamped, during the curricular reforms at the end of World War II, assigned a new name, moved into a distribution program, and, in the words of Horace, "perpetuates the traces of the ancient evil." The mind of the faculty, when personal interests are involved, can become unusually circumscribed.

The topical course has merit. Intrinsically it may possess the features of the distribution course in that it broadens the student's horizons and can evoke thought and a measured amount of research and investigation. Frequently, however, the student becomes the victim of the pursuit of knowledge for the sake of knowledge. There is little structural basis for subsequent courses in the field or area, and, while it can provide discipline in thinking which is a valuable concern also of the distribution course, it does little to arouse the student to a broad intellectual exploration, to bestir him to seek more, and to develop a perspective of all aspects of learning.

Finally the college is concerned, during the first two years, with the utilization of available teaching staff. The delicate area of maintaining high morale among students and faculty alike is pertinent here. Of even more immediate consequence is the matter of economy, as it arises from staffing elementary courses. Quality and quantity of a student's attainments developed in secondary school are graphically reflected in the number of sections scheduled in an elementary college course. The diversity of background would seem to call for diversity of sectioning until, carried to its theoretical extreme, the freshman course would resemble a tutoring operation where each student is a class unto himself. This situation is an expensive one, and it seems needless, though we can readily appreciate the upsurging need for more teachers, especially teachers who are qualified. At the same time we are not unaware of the fact that modern methods of testing emphasize a more vivid profile of a student, his potentialities, his knowledge, his attitudes—even the need to put him in a class by himself so far as a science or discipline is concerned. Nevertheless, take a subject like analytical geometry: what class procedure is to be followed when a third of those enrolled have presented for admission to college only algebra and plane geometry, while others have had trigonometry and solid geometry, and a few selected freshmen have had some experience with the calculus? The teacher of such a class is expected to progress with analytic geometry, imposing the uniformity of discipline upon students either not familiar with the ground rules of the subject or else so well prepared that the presentation of the subject stifles any motivation or incentive toward progress. The staffing of freshman sections differs from those of an upperclass course; in the latter it may be taken for granted that there is a uniformity of

educational experience, that the raw material which the Charter of
Brown University calls "the rising Generation" has already been
brought into some sort of conformity of mind and manners. Still,
the problems of assigning faculty to teach freshman courses (and
sophomores, too) can disrupt a departmental budget as new teachers
have to be added, generally at the last minute. These problems likewise can create a wall of indifference to the broad purposes of educational goals which may have been established. In the case of more
conscientious departmental chairmen who have to find staff for these
courses, these problems can even disrupt the lining of the stomach,
commonly referred to as ulceration.

We have, then, a set of problems ranging from the starry-eyed
collegiate applicant to the crass but essential reality of providing
teachers for lowerclass courses. The atmosphere of education is
generated by education out of the past, and any revolutionary attempt
to reform the system is met with two startling realities, conventionality and the indifference of public opinion. Conventionality feasts
upon tradition and roosts high enough to be untouchable in most
cases. Public opinion and advice can be aroused, but the resulting
"crash programs" invariably do more damage than good; moreover
"crash programs" frequently arise from misunderstood premises and
not from the heart of the matter.

These problems and the set of challenges which they imply have
provided the assumption upon which the curricula and the philosophy
of education at Brown University rest. Our thinking has been directed
to each of the problems which we have mentioned, and it is in the
solution of these that we have been experimenting with two curricula
during the last few years. Our problem is that of all education, but
it is the initiation of lowerclassmen into higher education that we
have found to be the most nettlesome but, at the same time, rewarding
study. Mentally and emotionally the graduate of a secondary school
comes to us with the response of the eighteen to twenty year old age
group. Our job has been to convert these students from uncoordi-
nated collectors of facts and impulses into scholars. In the process
we have endeavored to take account of such diverse elements as
experience and character, incorporating these into the design for a
prescription.

Environmental background may differ, circumstances of home and
school may vary, but each student is possessed of a mind capable of
development. In addition each freshman comes to college with a
complexity of feelings. Thus, while he is able to project himself

through activity that originates in the mind, he is also sensitive to the thoughts and opinions of others, whatever their age or generation. To stimulate this sensitivity and to evoke further mental and emotional responses to ideas should be the primary task of a lowerclass course. In many areas such stimulation should be defined as one of the goals of education. Looking at an education from a long range, we may say that without such stimulus a college education is for nothing. Unless the student is able to go forth into the world filled with a curiosity about everything around him, where he comes from and what he will do under any circumstance, we may say that his four years in college have been useless. It is most desirable that this stimulus should occur early in his college years, for then the work of college will animate his whole being and he will be in a spirit and in a mood to do something about himself. This stimulus of ideas may be called imagination, however much it is refined or representative of academic discipline.

Textbooks used in lowerclass and beginning courses may represent, we believe, a short-circuiting of this educational process. Lectures, while they can arouse the student's enthusiasm for a subject, likewise may hinder the student's response. The textbook and the survey lecturer will frequently impede the emotional and mental responses which are expected from the student. The author or the speaker edits and predigests the ideas of the original source, and while this is a very useful discipline in arousing the undergraduate's critical faculties through the use of these interpretive studies, we regard such interpretation as secondary to the chief end of immediate apposition with the original source. There are a number of books in which the problem of evil is explained, replete with quotations from Job through Kirkegaard. These books effect the identification of an idea—that there is evil in the world and that it can affect the good man. We say that the impression made by a reading of the Book of Job will have a greater impact upon the student than a book about the problem of evil. The student will seek to identify circumstances in his own life or that of others with the experiences of Job. The impression will be even more vivid as he reviews the nature of friendship, the power of money and good fortune, and the purpose of disease and suffering. He is free to interpret for himself; he is conditioned by no intermediary other than the impact of his fellow students who are undergoing the same experience and whose reactions he will naturally contrast, perhaps self-consciously, with his own.

In saying this, we have mentioned two kinds of response, the mental and the emotional. The lowerclassman displays these in predominant proportions. The mental, we insist, must be supplemented by the emotional, else the factor of personality will be negated at the expense of the purely rational. Without the emotional there is no room for the cultivation of tastes, a widening sense of appreciation, and accommodation of enthusiasm or inspiration, and the sheer matter of sympathy. These may be enhanced even as the mind is stimulated by the growing contacts between what the student already knows and what he is acquiring from these new and original sources.

There is however another response. This is not a natively endowed response but is one that comes during college work. This is the response of mental acquisitiveness, itself the result of the mental and emotional response. This response carries with it that overworked term "intellectual curiosity." To encourage intellectual curiosity has long been an aim of education. It was responsible for the break which Socrates made with the Sophists, and Aristotle with Plato. It is often cited in books about education; it is gallantly underscored in college catalogues. It is our experience that the student will be impelled to examine his idea further afield once he has been exposed to it. He will not be content with the solution which Job gives or does not give about the problem of evil. The experience of Job leads to an examination of the Christian version as found in the Gospels or the Greek version in Aeschylus and Sophocles, to the Roman concept embodied in Vergil's *Aeneid,* and on to Dante, Spinoza, Hume, Walter Lippmann, if you like. So much for isolated ideas in the religious-ethical sphere. But there is also a pertinence in the economic and political area, in the fields of science, be it disease or the indissolubility or destructiveness of matter.

In this mental acquisitiveness, then, in the application of the student's mind to the problems which have troubled many of the world's most significant thinkers, in the proper discipline of his emotions rests the stuff for the maturing process, at once both its cause and its effect. Through such an agent the transition between home and school and college is achieved effectively and smoothly. Since the mind, the emotions, and a desire to learn transcend this or that educational qualification, this or that curriculum, our lowerclassman proceeds with the same endowments as his classmates. So far as the college is concerned it is not necessary to operate a series of sections to accommodate the varying degree of preparation represented among its freshmen. These freshmen will be exposed, rather, to a discipline to which each brings himself as a human being, not as a graduate of this school or that academy, with this guidance director or that parent calling the tune.

Because the classics which are central to such a program represent in most instances a very fundamental exposition of the academic field or area in question, we consider them highly appropriate documents as introductory material. Some of the authors studied are the originating thinkers in an academic area, such as Freud for psychology, Adam Smith in economics, Malthus among sociologists. The fact that the subsequent development of an academic field has its origin predicated upon these classics is succeeded perhaps, in its educational value, only by the fact that class discussion and the student's own expanding interest and knowledge will lead to a reading of later thinkers upon that subject. To the concern expressed about adequate preparation, through such courses, for upperclass collegiate work, we must maintain that a perceptive mind and a contagious vigor for pursuing a subject beyond mere course commitments are the best conditions for upperclass work. The survey and the distribution course may instill facts and discipline, but an experimental course in ideas from a central classic will make the student weigh his facts and intelligently question his discipline. Faculty members will be the first to decry that concentrators within a subject are poorly prepared when they take up the major work. The same professor will be vocally assertive in his recognition that there is a hitherto unknown spirit of enthusiasm and eagerness about the campus—an enthusiasm and an eagerness for academic work.

These courses must likewise prevent the needless duplication of subject matter, a frequent weakness of lowerclass work, when considered alongside secondary school subjects. For the first time the lowerclassman will be confronted not only with systematic thinkers of first rank and the great minds in their particular academic fields, but also with an approach not found in secondary school. Since part of the purpose is to stimulate critical thinking and the role of subject matter is subordinated to philosophical content, the burden of these courses is with ideas as they exist in the classics. Not so long ago a young lady was asked in connection with the reading of the *Iliad* what she thought of the Greeks; her startled reply that she didn't know because she had not met any Greeks emphasizes the literal-minded outlook which some of these freshmen maintain upon entrance to college. At the end of the year that same young lady had developed to such a degree that she expressed the generous sentiment that the feminine sex was the root of all evil in the world and that Odysseus was truly the wisest and wiliest human being who ever lived. It is not without significance that she was recently seen on a date with a young man of Hellenic-American background.

We do not criticize the so-called "Great Books Course;" as it is found at Columbia and at St. John's College there is much to commend it. We must be wary, however, lest these great books be chosen for their subject matter alone or for their artistic form rather than for their ideas. In the light of conventional curricula the list of books may seem to some people rather bizarre. It is our feeling that a thorough study of Machiavelli's *The Prince* will disclose significant ideas to the student and will whet his critical appetite to a degree in which Karl Marx's *Das Kapital* and Hitler's *Mein Kampf* will seem ineffective in comparison. The book shelf, as we conceive it, should not be fixed. It cannot be set at 31 great books or even 100. Darwin's *Origin of Species* may yield to a collection of learned articles on genetics, but then there is also room for a Linnaeus or an Osler. A student exclaimed recently that he had worked out three completely irreconcilable concepts of Plato's philosophy as he read, cogitated, and discussed it in three different courses—in political science, in classics, and in philosophy. Call it initiation, imagination, or liberation, that student is getting an education.

Finally as this dilemma over Platonism clearly shows we believe that these courses will develop an appreciation of the unity that comes with diversity so far as the freshman-sophomore years are concerned. It has been stated that some academic programs permit the students to select as they choose so that their final assessment is a melange of everything in the college catalogue without a purpose, without a sense of academic design, least of all without an education. In a philosophical sense the lowerclassman is subjected to the science of metaphysics as he examines first principles, ways of knowing, and axiological standards. The pursuit and the evaluation of ideas admirably affect this. If Plato himself pointed the way to transcendentalism in his reference to the ascent from beautiful objects to beautiful concepts to beautiful relationships to the idea of beauty itself, he was not so much revealing the nature of mystical experience as he was underscoring the desirability of participation, something like the Aristotelian particular residing in the general and *vice versa*. If a course in the history of the fine arts can develop an interpretation of the Parthenon that differs from the interpretation worked out among classicists, we say "Good work!"—but our student of ideas will gradually perceive that the fundamental ideas are not merely aesthetic or documentary in nature;

they are at once economic and political and sociological. In the case of the Parthenon a potential rock doctor who has studied geology will have plenty more to contribute. It has been said that the whole science of economics can be summed up in one sentence: "there's no free lunch, boys;" yet philosophy is alleged to assuage the pangs of hunger, and the fine arts clearly show that man does not live by bread alone. We want our students to perceive the communalism of ideas and concepts and to examine each idea critically. The solution is not on the surface of the subject matter, the bond which unites all subjects in a common relationship. We want our lowerclassmen to plan for and to realize that unity which is central to all they learn.

To utilize the student's background of experience and attained knowledge out of home and secondary school, to provide him with enthusiasm and motivation for subsequent work within and after college, to stimulate a flow of ideas originating in the ideas of significant thinkers out of the past, and to preserve and to titillate and to augment the imagination of freshmen and sophomores—these we believe to be the essence of initiation into higher education. Problems in the transition between school and college will continue to aggravate administrators and teachers and parents and students as long as all parties resort to outmoded bloodletting instead of facing up to a proper diet which will purify the bloodstream. It is our conviction that the study of ideas in a few great thinkers, themselves the contributing founders of a science or discipline, provides more challenge than the rhetorical lecturer and the conventional textbook We are seeking motivation, and it can be found only when the freshman or sophomore finds it necessary to defend his own enlightened position, among his classmates, identifying and criticizing ideas

That the founding fathers of Brown University were aware of these transitional problems is amply attested in the University's Charter. We are thinking particularly of the phraseology "by forming the rising Generation" as this stands near the beginning of the document outlining the purpose of the original college. There is no reason to believe that pressures for admission and qualifications for entrance were less serious in the latter half of the eighteenth century than they are in the middle of the twentieth century. It is to the finished product, however, that the Charter looked then as indeed the University does now. Here there must be a perceptiveness into the first rudiments of human nature; youth has or will have great responsibilities; youth delights in the conventional but can be aroused to respond to the extraordinary; most people continue to act like youths throughout their lives unless this condition is corrected; opinion and knowledge, prejudice and truth are more frequently confounded than they are separated and identified. American educational institutions have turned out graduates of attainments and distinction, but the majority of graduates have emerged to fail to achieve anything startling or provocative, and, while there may be defects in character or personality which have gotten in the road of achievement, we find it impossible to dispel our belief that collegiate education in the past has not recognized its purpose and the appropriate commitments which this has involved.

III Pragmatic Development

"Man was made for employment. All his internal as well as external
powers testify to this great truth. To comply with this great dictate of
nature is of utmost importance; and youth, of all seasons of life, is the
fittest for this culture."
— JAMES MANNING, PRESIDENT, BROWN UNIVERSITY, 1789

The history of education presents ample evidence that instruction
may be either expository or participatory. Fundamentally these are
techniques in instruction; more significantly, however, they may
represent two separate attitudes toward a body of material or toward
knowledge. Principally the attitude is one of mentality, but the attitude
of the emotions in education can be equally accommodated in their
consideration.

By expository instruction we mean the manner of education which
establishes some authority whereby a student makes his judgments
and forms opinions about the subject matter under study. This
authority may assume various forms; it may be a textbook, a review
outline, a lecturer; even the weight of contemporary opinion may
serve to illuminate the subject to the student as he avidly pursues
what he assumes to be some form of truth, however remote from such
a criterion his labors prove to be. We are tempted to call this type
of learning "Roman," not merely because of its authoritative quality
and the function of some agent between the student and the subject
matter; it is Roman also because the student is exhorted to rise up
to some ideal which has been established by the judgment of years
as exemplary or the best of its kind. In its implications the ideal
is distinctive, not because of its own intrinsic merit, but because of
acceptance over the years and the *kudos* which it owes to cumulative
opinion. It is Roman because its transmission is effected by memorization and routine study, even as academic training in Classical
Rome consisted not of translating ideas and concepts into creative
effort but of learning facts of information for the sheer sake of knowing something and accumulating parts of knowledge. Furthermore,
it is in its encouragement—positive or negative—of value judgments
that expository education admits an association with the Romans;
it discourages relative thinking in its zeal to delineate what is truth

23

and what is its opposite; the student become addicted to a black-white, hot-cold way of examining evidence. Very little opportunity is provided for stimulating criticial sensitivity.

Participatory instruction, on the other hand, lacks in its process this authoritarian agent. If anything serves as a criterion for judgment, it is the student's reason and cumulative experience; at no time is a lecture or textbook held up to the student as the final authority. His knowledge is gained by his acquaintance with the source of his problem and the evidence available in the source. The student frames his judgment by reasoning upon a given body of material. His reasoning may be titillated through discussion with his contemporaries or other persons familiar with the subject. Fundamentally, however, he engages in a process of dialectic as he sifts, evaluates, and forms judgment upon his problem and its aspects. We might term this process of education "Greek," for it entails the probing and oral evaluation which characterize Greek thought as amply demonstrated in the Socratic dialogues of Plato. Less is said about truth or the final answer in this type of instruction than in the expository; emphasis is put on the cultivation of critical distinctions and the evaluation of evidence by the individual.

The distinction in procedure and technique which these two types of instruction represent is unfortunately never made clear to students as they move from secondary school to college; the problems raised are at the very heart of most of our educational problems. A child of grade school learns his multiplication tables, goes on to high school to learn about the right rules of rhetoric, chemical formulae, and the axioms of Euclid. His whole time is spent in two pursuits—learning authoritative rules which cover the ingredients of knowledge and accepting as final the judgment of his teacher or the writer of his textbook. If he is ever encouraged to question why or wherefore, he may be accused of bucking the system. He might be regarded as a sociological heretic or, what's worse, a juvenile delinquent of an intellectual order. It goes without saying that a great many of our most creative artists and scientists were the very ones who questioned the diet of authoritarianism and conventionality when they were in their formative educational years.

It was to substitute a greater degree of participatory instruction among other things in the curriculum at Brown that the Committee on the Curriculum voted to experiment with a number of courses in the program called the Identification and Criticism of Ideas, beginning with the academic year 1953-54. With this end in view, the two original premises of the program were established. First and foremost, the method of conducting classes was specified as one of free discussion about ideas, their evolution, their validity, and their pertinence to other ideas. In this connection, the role of the instructor was identified as that of a moderator of discussion, a mentor or a trainer who would supplement the students' discussion, framing the areas of discussion, guiding the analysis of ideas, but, in no sense of the word, providing value judgments about ideas except insofar as these were considered necessary for the maintenance of pertinent discussion.

The second premise concerned the subject matter of the experimental courses. The central text in each course was designated as some great classic or another, significant for its content as a work of literature as well as for its merit as a principal or inceptive document within an academic field or area. No predigested text or survey of a subject, the central classic was selected because it advanced an important and revolutionary set of ideas. As a qualification of this premise it may be stated that, while there might of necessity be other readings in the new courses, the ideas presented by an Aristotle, an Adam Smith, a de Tocqueville, or a Pavlov, each a significant originator of an area of study through the contribution of his ideas in the interpretation of life, these ideas were in themselves worthy enough to warrant analysis and critical evaluation. In the presentation of their ideas the authors of the classics were subject to the limitations which the laws of rhetoric and the written word impose upon creative thought. This, in itself, entails an area of scrutiny and interpretation which might demand supplementary reading.

In these two premises reside the uniqueness of the program and, at the same time, the actualizing agent of participatory education at Brown. These courses have been conceived of and are operated not as ordinary discussion courses; neither can they be classified as "great books" courses, though many of the central classics which have been adopted in the several courses are to be found among the "Great Books," and their ideas in the indices of the *Syntopticon*. We prefer to think of our courses as experimental in view of the fact that we have a well integrated standard curriculum of a distributive nature. But, in essence, the experimental nature of these courses is no transitory phenomenon; they express our conviction, not only that a curriculum must be constantly kept in a state of evolution, but, more particularly, that the heart of the curriculum must contain such an inquiry into values which is a procedure as old as Socrates,

Cicero, Quintilian, Ascham, as modern as Whitehead, Wriston, and Highet.

When we say that these are no ordinary discussion courses, we hasten to add that discussion is not merely the expression of intellectual rhetoric. Hamlet's sardonic comment, "Words, words, words," is meaningful in this day of increased ease of communications and of advertising media, when students seem encouraged to discuss matters in terms which are either irrelevant or impertinent. The students have plenty of opinions, and opinion has always been a nuisance in the development of the mind, of reason, and of knowledge. Opinion, however, once tested and tried in the crucible of debate fired with the stabilizing flame of a great document, admirable for its articulativeness as for its implications, this refined opinion begins to attain the stature of knowledge. It is perhaps a good thing that American students are all so anxious to have discussions. It is part of our tradition; it has been nurtured in the town meeting, at the family hearth, in the locker room, and in the dormitory lounge. This exchange of what are termed "ideas" occurs on platforms, radio, and TV screens. Students are zealous in demanding panels at undergraduate conferences. Congress and the legislators provide models of discussion. Discussion is at the very heart of our judicial process.

When discussion lacks conviction, it dies of its own weight. Simply to hold discussions for the sake of discussion has little to commend it. It has been our experience, however, that discussion based upon the ideas set forth by a figure who has wrestled firsthand with some of the ethical and philosophical problems of human beings is a form of mental discipline as effective in the sphere of systematic training as it is in recreative criticism. The student is faced with a set of principles, of ideas, of convictions which bring forth a response based on his own experience and attitudes. To identify what is and what is not an idea is a discipline in and by itself useful in the development of his own scholarship. To perceive the relation of one idea to another and their association with the concept or thesis of the author is an ideal of education which we believe stimulates the imaginative projection of the student and his own dialectic. Always it is discussion arising from the text of the great classic that actualizes this process.

As a moderator of the discussion in one experimental course, the teacher is conceived of as a person of some intellectual and spiritual sensitivity who has the ability to determine the course of reason which the discussion of ideas is assuming or following. His background must be broad, for he may be called upon to witness any and all ramifications of the field in which a central classic is being analyzed, but he must also be a scholar familiar with the implications of scholarship. The teacher has the responsibility, also, to see that the discussion does not lapse into eristic on the one hand or into pure divagation, the bull session, without purpose on the other. Above everything else, his familiarity with the implications of the central classic must be contagious, for he will be thrust into the midst of an enthusiastic and virtually devastating discussion of the author and the author's thesis.

At an early point in the development of our program it was specified that the instructor of an IC course (as courses in the Identification and Criticism of Ideas are popularly referred to) should keep with his section for the whole academic year. In effect, we are saying that the impact of personality looms large in the development of the student. Not only does the student mature more effectively when he is subjected to a whole academic year of analyzing ideas and the civilizing effect such a concentration upon metaphysics can create. From his classmates and the moderator he will acquire also a respect for values—social and intellectual—quite easily lost in the limited containment of the normal one-semester course. There is no small irony in attempting to semesterize two millennia of thinking upon a problem like the role of the emotions in daily conduct. We believe that one academic year will better equip the student to perceive deeper facets of the emotional, let alone define emotion, when his thoughts are directed upon this problem with a Freud or an Ovid or a Croce as a guide under a moderator, aware of the implications and general areas of concentration of this problem, and in the presence of classmates whose views may differ from his own.

At the beginning of the program attention was focused upon the number of students these classes should contain. Postwar collegiate enrollment in lecture courses and classes provided part of the answer. While masses of students can be put through the academic mill with lecture-courses and a host of graduate assistants to read essays and correct homework and hour tests, the atmosphere is not the most effective way to stimulate thinking—creative or systematic. An inspiring lecturer can arouse students, as we have stated, but who will follow up the cultivation of enthusiasm? The small preceptorial section of seven to ten students seems most desirable, but this has its drawbacks, not only in the expense involved in faculty personnel, but, more particularly, in the exclusiveness and preciousness which is likely to be fostered. The figure of 20 was arrived at as the most appropriate number of students in a class. With 20 students there was a broader opportunity for diversity of background to emerge and to nurture discussion. Illness and absenteeism would have less effect upon the discussion and development of theme in a class of 20. Finally, while we are sympathetic toward a sensible exclusiveness that must befit a community of scholars, we felt that classes of less than 20 students, particularly in an experimental program, would foster the attitude and thinking of a mutual admiration society.

The effectiveness of the class of 20 in the IC program has been proven as the program progresses. In fact, in a few instances where conflict of class hours, ineligibility of candidate for enrollment, and the sudden creation of new sections under pressure of a course's popularity have served to depreciate the optimum of 20, the lacuna has had a demoralizing effect upon the spirit and the participation of the class. Our specified number of 20 as well as the fact that the whole program is to a degree optional have worked together to obviate a divided student body, a charge frequently heard in the stages of planning this curriculum, as the students pursue separate courses of study in their early years of college in their initiation into higher education. Among 20 the strong, silent person is more likely to speak up than among 30; among 20 the aggressive spouter can be properly handled by his associates. Among 20 it has been found that the developing perspective in discussion is enhanced, the topics of assigned oral reports can achieve adequacy of coverage, and there can be an intellectual exhilaration not commonly found in the undergraduate classroom.

As for stage properties, the conventional arrangement of the classroom was found not suitable. The rows of arm-desk chairs facing the desk of the instructor in the front of the room are not conducive to discussion. In fact, the thought of holding discussion among students who have their backs one to another is ironic, however effective discussions may be in some circumstances. Conviction commands the whole personality when the student can look his associates in the eye. Moreover, psychologists report that a student's response is one of greater assurance if he can grasp a table in front of him when he begins to speak! To this end, tables were arranged in a hexagon and the students and instructor are thus able to see each other at all times. The novelty of this plan of seating, while it was an innovation to meet a specific purpose, has gained acceptance also in language classes at Brown and, in some instances, it has been found useful for graduate seminars. The visual facility that the hexagonal arrangement provides, we feel, is superior to that of the conference table where there must of necessity be craning of necks to see or be seen. It has been discovered that these IC tables prevent students from huddling into groups or from assuming squatters' rights in one preferential location if the instructor sits at a different place class by class.

As if to give the new program an even chance of success as an educational experiment, the enrollment was opened in the first year of operation to those prospective sophomores who stood in the upper half of their class and to freshmen of similar standing as forecast by their natural IQ CEEB scores, and class rank in secondary schools. A few shills from the lower half of the classes were admitted to IC courses to assist in prognosticating expansion of qualifications of eligibility. That the new set of courses aroused popular interest is underscored by the clamor to enter the program. Subsequently, the specification of "upper half" was amended to include the "upper two-thirds" of the classes. Time, the success of the venture, and enthusiasm in all quarters have made the courses available to all students; at least two of these courses are required of every student in his first two years. This adjustment anticipated a future broadening of the eligibility rules to comprehend any student who desires to enter the program. Some students, though eligible for the experimental courses, preferred to pursue the standard distributive curriculum. Many others in the standard course of study have succeeded in entering the IC program. Enthusiasm for the program and faith in its integrity have led the faculty more recently to incorporate it with the standard program into a new curriculum. This is a vindication of the fact that any student can pursue courses in the experiment, as indeed each student will be required to do.

Gratifying has been the response in the skeptical student who manifested a "show me" attitude in the barrage of publicity concerning discussion of the nature and consistency of ideas. Again, the most stalwart defender and victim of expository education has had his renaissance in the adoption of stimulated and independent study. We can cite many examples of the "C" student who has surpassed his more gifted brethren in the upper half of the class by zealous performance in IC classes and the realization, not only in our tests and examinations when he was a sophomore, of a heightened maturity as he went on into a field of upperclass concentration. Some few of these have actually improved their academic rank in the sophomore year and through the rest of their college career by their participation in experimental courses.

There is, of course, the problem of the dour student who shrinks from participating in the discussion which occurs in his IC courses. Any attempt to go to work on him by his associates or the instructor is met by a terse "Yes" or "No." These strong, silent types generally do a good job on class reports, essays, and examinations. In all fairness should these students be permitted to take up room when others with greater gifts of articulation are excluded once the limit of enrollment has been met? This question is even more pertinent, as all students are now required to take experimental courses. Our answer to it is definitely in the affirmative. We regard it, first of all, as a challenge to the skillful instructor to motivate the participants in such a way that student indifference, actual or feigned, will be dispersed. If the trouble is an anti-social attitude, the other participants may help to dispel this. Secondly, this may be the only occasion these students will ever have in all their educational experience of being exposed to thinking for themselves; conversation is not always a concomitant of the thinking process. Finally, we have not cited perfection as a premise for the experimental courses. Were this perfection possible we would be able to cap the Seal's pyramid on the reverse of the dollar bill. Our purpose is to stimulate ideas, not to form the whole man, however much we may assist in the process; time and nature alone will take care of that; we can only hope to expedite the development. There are slow and cautious starters; there are many thoughtful people who are reluctant to express their convictions. We must assess the silent student, not alone in the terms of the requirements for a baccalaureate as he makes the transition from parental dominance to his own intellectual self-mastery, but, more especially, for that occasion in his life when a great decision that he must make entails both precise thinking and articulate expression. Well adjusted people can be boring; but, when they are well adjusted undergraduates, they can be deadly.

The technique of conducting these participatory courses is limited only as the imagination of the instructor and the participants and the nature of the central classic can be contained. A potential ideal was proposed a little while ago when a veteran instructor in IC courses asserted that an alumnus of this program should be able to develop a systematic train of ideas upon any concept or term in the English language; this train of ideas, he elaborated, must lend itself to humanistic adaptation, that is, it must admit cognizance of the questions, "What is Man?" and "What is his relation to his Creator, his fellow men, and the material world around him?" This certainly implies a pregnant imagination on the part of the student, but the imagination, however lively, must be conditioned by critical evaluation in the sphere of the mental and in the sphere of taste by the response of emotional validity.

The fact that the experimental courses are scheduled for an academic year rather than for one semester assists in developing temporal and intellectual perspective. Reports can be assigned in September for oral delivery as late as the following April or May. This not only increases the sense of perspective in the student; it enhances the cohesiveness of the course, as indeed does also the central classic. A panel or jury designated to criticize or evaluate these reports or, more pertinently, the sources whence they are derived enlivens, we have found, the class procedure. The presentation by groups of students of a debate over interpretation of some principle in the central classic emphasizes the teamwork which the experimental courses provide and debating has the further faculty of clarifying or enlarging implications, as it were, through dialectic.

We believe that there is a very real place for written and oral reports in the first two years of college. There is the element of research which goes into the preparation of these. Just as important, however, is the exercise in evaluation and shifting of evidence which research involves. Of similar significance is the matter of practice in expression and of exercise in criticism that involves other members of the class. This combats the sterility which a lowerclass program of studies frequently entails. This quickens the maturing process between secondary school and university scholarship. This makes for that incentive which the present generation of college students needs if the tradition of learning is to maintain any perspective into the future.

There are instances in IC courses of the three areas, humanities, social studies, and science, where students contribute short lectures, supplementary to the main reading and discussion of the course. That these brief discourses meet with an enthusiastic and provocative response from students is indicative of the potential which lectures in distribution courses possess for eliciting students' reactions—a potential, we might add, rarely actualized in the conventional lecture or class. In another sphere they point up the significant role which objective presentation of a thesis has in a course of study that is singularly subjective in its approach. Transferred to an IC course in which creative work is a substantial part of the year's assignment, this type of presentation is perhaps the most invaluable aspect of the whole training of the future writer or artist. An IC course in poetry or the fine arts or music, therefore, would seem to insure the germane training of the prospective artist or critic and insure it within the general area of a liberal arts education. Here is an audience which can react sympathetically, yet firmly; a board of critics sharing a mutual training in the principles of art or of crafts, yet critics whose personal experience has been broad enough to allow for the development of taste, a factor of no small consequence.

Because of the intensive nature of these participatory courses and the opportunity afforded the student to demonstrate his knowledge and attainments at each meeting of the class, hour tests and examinations assume proportions different from those in the conventional lowerclass course. The exploratory essay has been found to possess unusual pertinence and adaptability in these courses. Unlike the conventional discussion questions in the hour tests or examinations of a standard course, the exploratory essay of an IC course does not seek alone to test the student's acquisition of facts and the interpretations of these. The emphasis rather is directed toward stimulating in the student the desire to utilize knowledge he has gained in reading and discussion and reflection as the basis for interpreting some meaningful idea out of his own experience and that of the ages. At all times interpretation and the seasoned conclusion are of the essence and, for pedagogical purposes, most significant. The conventional hour test in these experimental courses draws away from time well spent in the oral exploration of ideas. Unless the hour test can be so designed as to elicit a provocative response from the student, we hold that an oral test is preferable.

Traditionally, the final examination is the parade ground for facts, oddments of information, and other miscellanea, which the students sense to be either important or indicative of professorial scholarship or caprice. This makes for two reactions. First of all, students will cram, will read outlines, will seek tutors, will even look inside encyclopedias in their zeal to beat out the professor at his own game—all of this generally within 48 hours of the final examination. In these terms, the final examination can become nothing more than an exaggerated demonstration, not of knowledge, but of what students think the professor wants them to know. Secondly, and perhaps more important, a final examination may foster in the student a dogmatic belief that there can be a final answer in every aspect of the course of study. To actualize this erroneous assumption, the student reduces whole centuries, whole traditions, and whole creative processes to a table or a paradigm of highlights, important points, "cold dope," call it what you like. His written answers will seek to expand and embellish these facts into an organic whole, symbolic of the final answer on the subject, while in reality there may be no final answer and any attempt to give one is as fallacious as the mentality that sees learning in this light of questions and answers.

It is hardly necessary here to belabor the whole question of relevancy in so far as questions are answered on examinations. Evidence is more than plentiful in a conventional examination that a student who has mechanically crammed paradigms and outlines on the eve of the examination will substitute almost defiantly what he has learned for what the examiner specifically is requesting. "Vergil was a famous Roman poet, but there are six aspects of humanism in the odes of Horace. These I will now discuss . . . ." All this has an old familiar ring, when the examiner sought to find out the nature of human destiny in Vergil's *Aeneid*. Deviation and divagation, these are fostered by the conventional hour test and final examination. These along with the injudicious use of "background material," i.e., setting the large canvas for the answer to the question which generally is never apparent —these are no longer problems when the student is rehearsed in ideas, when he has had practice in isolating and criticizing ideas. A final examination in the liberal tradition can never be a rehearsal of facts and information; rather it becomes for the student a written experience in critical analysis with personal appraisal and the exercise of taste. As one of our instructors has shown, a final examination consisting of one question in the form of an essay, in which a selected passage from a philosopher is presented for a full commentary and analysis, proved a greater stimulus to an original intellectual workout than the reams of conventional spot passages and identifications of terms and situations we associate with customary final examinations in philosophy or in any subject, for that matter.

An analysis made of the study habits of students in one IC course before and after the mid-year and final examinations emphasizes the calm, rational approach these students were able to maintain toward the examinations. They realized that cramming, "No-doz"-ing and the use of other forms of barbiturates were out of the question in view of the nature of the term's work. Absent were lecture notes, drug store outlines, and other accumulations of academic greengroceries that are best buried in fraternity files. Each student admitted that he or she read again the central classic in preparation for the examination—a final reading that was both thought-provoking and reflective. Inevitable is the experience that the more frequent the perusal the more iridescent the lines of thought-communication reveal themselves to be—all of this, after a term or a year of discussion. One or two students signified that they extracted single sentences from the work at random and practiced short, three-sentence critiques of these passages. Still others developed analyses of nouns and adjectives pertinent to the pattern of the author's ideas. This is not a stunt; it is the development within the students of the art of self-mastery and of clear thinking. It is an aspect of participatory education which we regard most highly.

As for time and class hours, most of the IC courses were fitted upon inception into the characteristic three meetings a week of 50 minutes each. Herein the program conformed with the scheduling of all undergraduate instruction at Brown. At an early point it was common experience that these conventional periods were found to be too short for full expansion of potential discussion—"the time is always up, sir, just when we get a really good discussion going." This is something of a contrast to the age-old "saved by the bell" tradition. It has been found that two weekly periods of 75 minutes each assist in maintaining these discussions and augmenting the spirit of inquiry. In one or two instances the class meets for three hours one afternoon or evening a week with a short recess at mid-point. It may seem unctuous to acknowledge that informal conversation during the recess has proved to be an extension of the class discussion. It does signify, however, that the students have been fired up with what they are doing. One IC course in science experimented with one or two hour sections a week (a separate laboratory period made up the full assignment of four hours in science) and it was found that this hampered the students' expansiveness in discussion. That there are certain psychological sanctions at work in the scheduling as well as in the staging of the IC class is evident.

Intellectual curiosity is a phrase of much usage. It is proclaimed from the commencement platform in secondary schools as the graduates leave that phase of their education. In college it has become a cliche popular with the administration when social and athletic activity would eclipse the academic; with counselors and advisers to arouse motivation; for athletes it is a symbol that there is often something higher in the spiritual sphere; for alumni it is an idea of general agreement as long as it can be confined in space and time and does not cost too much. Why is there such fascination for this phrase, and wherein does it persist? Once uttered, it retreats into the cosmos.

There is, we believe, in all men a latent belief, conscious or unconscious, in the endless quest for full knowledge. It is summarized poignantly in Socrates' appraisal of his own reputation among men when he admitted the charge of wisdom on the grounds that he did not know, and hence alone was wise. At one time or another every individual is brought to realize that the process of learning has no end; such a momentary realization may well be defined as maturity. To accelerate this belief and to actualize it is the goal of most educators. It is a goal that is generally obscured by the simple aspects of living; textbooks patently hinder the process by their omniscient containment; lecturers are so frequently carried away by their rhetoric that their subject matter is taken to be the final word; means of communication like radio and television abound in quiz shows whose general effect is to pronounce absolutely between the right and wrong answers (and here a departure from academic procedure exists, *viz.* the wrong answer brings a consolation prize in the form of a Cadillac.)

In another phase, this cliché of "intellectual curiosity" may signify a state of inadequacy, of intellectual sterility; it is a phrase of desperation pronounced when all other forms of momentary incentive and motivation have failed. A teacher can recommend a volume to a student, but unless that student is innately receptive to this form of recommendation the chances are he will never read the book. We believe that the atmosphere can and must be created where the intellectual curiosity arises within the young person himself; to this end no manual of instructions is necessary. Participatory education is the only form of instruction we know of in the conventional span of educational experience from kindergarten to senior year in college where this atmosphere can prevail. Only in recognition of this will intellectual curiosity cease being merely a cliché or a well-intentioned attitude.

IV Teachers Instead of Pedagogues

"If your scholar do miss sometimes, chide not hastily; for that shall both dull his wit, and discourage his diligence; but monish him gently; which shall make him both willing to amend and glad to go forward in love and hope of learning." — ROGER ASCHAM

Characteristic of the Age of Enlightenment, the Charter of Brown University emphasizes the intellectual commitment of the institution in a distinction between the "learned faculty" and the "teaching faculty." To the Board of Fellows was assigned the general policy of education; they comprised the learned faculty in their concern with the curriculum, with the academic climate, and with what might be termed the prevailing scholarly morale. The teaching faculty was given the responsibility of imparting knowledge, maintaining a high level of morality in the college, and of provoking among the students "a generous disposition for thought." If, then, the Fellows were to be the architects of the plan and the course of study, representing as they did persons of eminence and professional qualification in the community and the Colonies, it was the obligation of the members of the faculty not merely to recreate the students in the image of greatness which resided in the Fellows, but there was an even greater responsibility to implement the established curricula and policies with perspective and imagination. The teacher of 1764, if we can gauge the behavior and the spirit of the students from some of the legislation on the college's books, had to be "a man honored for noble character and service who with speech could sway their passion and soothe their troubled hearts."

Of pertinent significance is the Charter's emphasis upon the plan of study and the designation of the agents in this matter. Of significance, also, is its concern with the role of instruction, its perspicacious observations about the quality of the governing bodies, the students, and the graduates. No commonplace document, this Charter was conceived and written with the accent on greatness, be it in the designation of the two faculties or in the emphasis on "usefulness and reputation" which are mentioned as goals and ends of the undergraduate education. To arouse the students to greatness, to bestir their sights above the mediocrity of their former pursuits to the new roles which society and science together demanded of them, and finally to enkindle a desire for learning, for acquiring information, not for what it represents in terms of usefulness, but for what it can effect upon the mind of the scholar, what might be called intellectual incentive—these are the goals of education as they are handed down from another century in the form of this Charter.

If the history of education tells us anything, it underscores in dramatic terms the tremendous role of the teacher. It is a role, however, that is not limited solely to terms of assessment of information imparted. In few instances are we informed about the subject matter that was taught. The effectiveness of the great teacher is expressed not as much in subject matter as in the terms of the enthusiasm which he possesses and the conviction with which he transmits this contagious spirit to his pupils. Plato was but one of a small group enkindled by Socrates, and the large corpus of Platonic dialogues remains as a tangible token of the invigorating impact of the teacher upon pupil. For Aristotle, in turn, Platonic incentive became the starting point of a career teeming with enthusiasm for learning, as he was fired up to enquire into the nature of some Platonic premises and from these to proceed to the ultimate expression of a new philosophy. The Christian religion has sought to realize this zeal in the missionary movement as it fanned out to and from the disciples and apostles; yet again the personality of the Teacher and the example of His life transcend many aspects of doctrine as a source of inspiration. Once the convictions and enthusiasm of Christianity flagged and the Church settled back to live secure in its temporal institutions it took another group of teachers and interpreters to utilize the discovery of Greek as a means of arousing new ideas, new ways of interpretation, and to revolutionize thinking and action. It was a Ficino or an Erasmus or a small group of scholars at Paris or in Cambridge, who were the enthusiastic teachers whose contagious zeal was commuted to others.

The late Dean Andrew Fleming West of Princeton used to say that the chief end of graduate training was not so much the pursuit of knowledge as it was the establishment of a climate in the soul that would demand intellectual satisfaction. While foundations and educators express concern over the growing shortage of teachers in America and new schemes are put into practice to alleviate this shortage through more astute employment of available faculty, there is little question that the chief source of attraction into the academic ranks is the teacher himself. This source of attraction may be considered in two aspects.

It can be actualized first in the wake of enthusiasm for the subject which he teaches and which he passes along to his students. There is a source of attraction also in the admiration for the teacher as a human being. There is a presence, above any manner of teaching or method of instruction, that the teacher can manifest, and this can animate the student to emulation, scholastic or otherwise; hence our concern for the role of the faculty in the development of an undergraduate curriculum. We posit the faculty, therefore, as the most important entity in any academic institution, above the library, above the real estate assets of the college, above the student body itself—it is the faculty that makes the institution worthy of its professed purposes. There is ample evidence that continuation of the tradition is most successfully accomplished by the faculty.

Brown is perhaps unusual in its status as one of the few university-colleges in America. The faculty of the College and of Pembroke is also the faculty of the Graduate School. This means that the distinction made at some institutions between a teaching faculty and a research faculty becomes at Brown merely a scheduling incidental. The teacher who can motivate an undergraduate to select a field of concentration and who can fire him with enthusiasm for a subject or a field of study must possess a similar capacity to exploit the potentialities of the graduate student in the field of contemporary research, in methods that are new and that indicate the sensitivity of the teacher to his own obligation as a participant in research. To maintain this balance in the choice of a faculty is difficult, but it has been our conviction that the two functions cannot be separated. An endowed teacher sometimes is not concerned about research or even in instructing graduate students in a bare detail like the bibliography in his subject. Similarly, a first-rate scholar on occasion may find it almost a violation of principle to comprehend the vitality of an expanding interest in research into an appropriately meaningful synthesis for the beginner in the field. It is our belief that the great scholar can very definitely contribute to the maturing process of the undergraduate. How else will the undergraduate be stimulated in his respect for scholarship? For graduate students, also, it is felt that there will be tangible benefits if the scholar has acquired the knack of articulation and tolerance that must figure in undergraduate presentation. We hardly need to add that the urbanity and appreciative acumen which signify the teacher of undergraduates can certainly not harm graduate students. This takes on a certain poignancy when a certain eminent mathematician describes his colleagues as those who eat with a knife and fork and those who use their fingers.

The introduction of any new curriculum or the modification of any established academic procedure will create two phenomena among a faculty: (1) change will always elicit a howl of anguish from one or more members; (2) the proposal for something new has a tendency to thrust into prominence someone who by training or inclination or past performance seems peculiarly adapted to take on a particular assignment. In one sense, these phenomena are regrettable, for divisiveness can detract from the purpose of the institution, which is instruction. But when a faculty like that at Brown has a long tradition of harmony, a new curriculum can serve principally to arouse interest, create discussion, and enkindle an anticipation for something new in operation. If any question is raised, it will not be so much which person is qualified to teach that course—the scholar, the enthusiastic teacher, or the experimentalist in a department—as it will be how fully a department can embark upon the new program and to what degree must a department be enlarged if it is to cooperate in the proposed plan of study.

When the experimental program in the Identification and Criticism of Ideas was proposed, the question arose not about graduate versus undergraduate faculty, for here there was no distinction; rather, since sections of these new courses were to be limited to 20 students and it seemed desirable to continue course offerings in the standard curriculum, the problem became one of economics and time-motion study. The Carnegie Corporation very generously solved the former with a grant to underwrite the program for five years. This grant enabled the University to bring new faculty members to the campus, both to participate in the experimental curriculum and to fulfill teaching commitments in the standard curriculum in so far as the regular faculty undertook assignments in experimental courses.

That the greatest responsibility of the collegiate administration lies in its choice of a faculty was amply demonstrated in the difficult task of adding new teachers who, by their qualifications, would achieve the most effective assimilation into established faculty ranks. This question, then, how to increase the teaching staff without disturbing the prevailing philosophy of education and at the same time without provoking division in the ranks, is at the very heart of any experimental program where a faculty is concerned. What has been most heartening in this connection is the complete absence of cleavage; fears were expressed that a curriculum which, at the outset at least, was to be pursued by a certain number of qualified students would encourage a comparably elite faculty. This never materialized and the reason is that the new members were sought expressly as regular members of the faculty; likewise, older teachers who entered the IC program did so frequently in the conviction that this program had exploratory merits, that it was an experiment, and that all comparisons of its practicality had of necessity to be made in the light of the existing curriculum, itself one which had been devised immediately after World War II.

The nature and the composition of the faculty have a pertinence to effective undergraduate instruction. We believe that the first qualification of a teacher is one of personality. Personality is interpreted not merely in terms of the enthusiasm that the teacher brings to his subject in the presence of his students; it means, also, the facility of communicating to the students in their own language, in terms they can grasp, while at the same time elevating their perspective above the conventional. It can mean, also, participation in the world of the student, as the student responds to the maturing process. Maturity in the undergraduates may be promoted by research and assignments but, in the final analysis, we believe that associations with the instructor will prove to be the most effective agent in the maturing process. It is not so much a question of imparting knowledge that we must insist upon in the role of the faculty member; we believe, rather, that the student should have intimate contact with the academic personality. The small class in which discussion constitutes the approach to a subject can facilitate this intimacy, with benefits too numerous to mention on both sides, in a way no closed TV circuit and no formalized lecture can ever achieve. In terms of moderating classes in the experimental curriculum, the personality of the instructor is highly significant: it can provide the incentive for student participation at the beginning of the year; it is a responsible factor for creating an atmosphere conducive to the analysis of ideas and concepts; above everything else, it is the personality of the instructor that can prevent a trend of ideas from becoming so academic as to lose human pertinence. By the latter we do not suggest that the instructor has an obligation to interfere with the natural criticism of ideas, let alone their analysis; but we maintain that the cumulative experience of an older human being can inject the necessary dimension of humanity into an argument or thesis which develops along logical, but sometimes quite unrealistic, lines. The personality of the instructor will be to his advantage in such an instance.

The scholarship of a faculty member is virtually as important as his personality. That the teacher possess a doctorate or at least be within sight of this degree is essential, for a thorough knowledge of the field of study is guaranteed in part by the discipline which work for this degree entails. This familiarity with a subject is necessary for moderating IC classes. Without graduate training the teacher may manifest certain virtues in aesthetic criticism, and he may be perfectly capable in conducting a class where procedure consists of reviewing superficially daily assignments. But a class in ideas demands more than simple familiarity with the letter of the assignment. It implies an extensive knowledge of the whole field—an erudition which has become a part of the individual, proficiency that transcends mere facts and will represent seasoned judgment that can come only with experience in the widening horizons of scholarship. Moreover, the study of ideas, whether it consists of identifying or of analyzing them, is nothing but a form of metaphysics, an investigation into first principles, be it considered as causation, phenomenology, influence, or transmission. It is only through extensive immersion in the problems of scholarship that a good teacher can be pronounced effective in his role.

Publication and research are, therefore, perhaps even more significant than the mere qualifications of advanced degrees. To have participated in the widening boundaries of knowledge through research and to have recorded articulatively the results of research will sharpen the teacher's presentation of his subject. Over and above any considerations of the expansion of knowledge or of the *kudos* which is the author's and, in some instances, his institutions's, publication can exploit in dramatic way an orderliness of mind and adjustment of mind to expression which are invaluable to the classroom. This is especially desirable when instruction occurs in a course on ideas. If one goal of a good teacher is to make his students mentally alert and critical, it is imperative that he himself have experience in the test of scholarly judgment. Possibly the best such test comes not in his oral examination for the doctorate but in a series of rejection slips for a learned article, the product of considerable research on his part but still subject to a higher judgment of his peers.

What administrative officials frequently overlook, as additions are made to a faculty, is the amount of teaching experience a teacher brings to his new position. The statement is often made that there is nothing as arrogant as a young Ph.D. in his first teaching position. Alumni may recall with some disdain the young instructor in English who knew all the answers, whose discipline was completely ineffective, and who was a total failure at teaching a class, let alone motivating his students to anything but disgust. One alumnus of some attainments has reported that since graduation he has never been able to read or witness *Romeo and Juliet* after an experience he had as a freshman with a young Ph. D. The impression that alumnus had of Shakespeare could be expressed only in terms of Kittredge, Bradley, and J. Dover Wilson. That English instructor is now an actuary. He's probably an expert in his field, too. The instructor with his facile knowledge of all the end-tests in Shakespeare was still unable to communicate anything in a positive sense to the undergraduates before him.

Now an administrative staff that is chiefly academic, one that co-operates with the departments of learning in the designation of new faculty, is the most positive safeguard against the appointment of these academic uncommunicados. It is not without reason that many administrative staffs require that prospective young faculty shall have put in some time either in a high school or a preparatory school where class discipline and the effective articulation of ideas have been gotten across at a level which is even more difficult than at the freshman-sophomore level in college, for secondary teaching can round off the sharp edges that come with bibliography and other detail of advanced graduate work. A conventional procedure is that younger faculty members shall work up through the ranks, mainly by handling sections of classes and correcting papers as graduate students. There is much to be said for this, but we also find that in this procedure there is a boredom which is anything but inspiring for the young person and an experience which may sour him about the whole academic life as he prepares to enter the field professionally. Then, too, there are young instructors who, for lack of motivation, decide to leave the academic groves and enter business life, a sure indictment of some aspects of the system as well as of themselves.

In academic life the inaccurate cliché is often heard that the good teacher rarely publishes and that the publishing teacher fails to arouse his students or provide them with incentive. In most institutions of learning this can lead to tragedy. We can only hope for the ideal situation where mature and publishing scholars are sufficiently aroused about their several commitments, *viz.* that knowledge is not stagnant and that expansion is achieved in a variety of ways. Entirely too much discussion has been made about the eternal academic dilemma of teaching *vs.* research, for the teacher surrounded with the ingredients of scholarship in the preparation for his classes will derive an impulse toward scholarship as he surveys the facets of his field which are incomplete. The writer of learned articles, likewise, should be the first to observe the blank looks from his students when he fails to be as communicative orally as he is in the well documented yet readable treatise.

Personality and scholarship, therefore, we hold to be the most essential aspects of the good teacher, but if there are the generalized qualifications that we look for in university teachers we may also add that there are other aspects of the profession desirable in the picture of the teaching faculty.

When the experimental program in the Identification and Criticism of Ideas was first proposed, one of the stipulations was that a faculty member should devote his whole teaching schedule to his IC course. The thinking behind this proposal reasoned that the teacher was, in a sense, to model the course as he deemed such a course should be presented. It was felt that without the encumbrance of other teaching commitments the IC instructor could concentrate upon the projection of ideas which were likely to develop in his course. Since each department participating in the experiment satisfied itself with only one or two IC courses, the instructor's schedule consisted of three sections for this course. We still believe that this scheduling is the ideal arrangement, but no one was able at that time to foresee the burgeoning of IC courses within a department and the popular demand for new courses, some of them consisting of only one or two sections. The exclusiveness of a teacher's schedule in IC work enabled the experiment to get the full treatment. The only complaint voiced in this original stipulation was the lack of contact which the IC instructor had with the other courses and affairs in his department.

It is certainly true that departmental matters are a source of interest, something comparable to the incidental intelligence purveyed in a boarding house. To this we say simply that some instructors are unable to rise above the atmosphere of graduate school where each appointment or advancement comes in for a thorough discussion among the assembled brethren. We are not loathe to grant that an IC instructor should be thoroughly familiar with what is done in other departmental courses. But the instructor who is keen and enthusiastic about his course in ideas, living and recording his scholarship, will be fully cognizant of those significant advances which occur among his colleagues and which are of general academic concern. The impact of the IC courses or of any good academic program does not admit of evaluation in terms of hours or of schedules; this is the matter for the recorder who is paid to keep track of such commitments.

We aver that there can be no such thing as a nine-to-five faculty. At Oxford a neat but subtle distinction is made between a professor "of Oxford" and one "at Oxford." This distinction says much about the behavior of academicians; it can be interpreted many ways, but in this higher academic life it vindicates the great devoted teacher at the expense of the instructor who meets students at appointed times. While it is true that these courses meet three times a week in the classroom, that cannot be taken as a measure of the teacher's responsibilities; the charge must continue beyond the confines of the classroom: the coffee lounge, the pub, the instructor's office, the professor's residence. This is the very reason for the residential concept in education and not all of the potentialities in this respect have yet been explored. It is at the basis of the great preparatory schools and has been cited as one of the chief reasons for the continuing popularity of these schools. It is commonly accepted as a virtue of the collegiate institution in the eastern part of the United States. It is a matter which knows no distinction of private or public endowment. It is a mark of real liberal education and it has been the salvation of many an institution. We can cite one out of many examples at Brown where the whole system of associate fellows for student residences has been sparked by one eminent teacher as gracious in his duties as a chaperone at undergraduate dances as he is enthusiastic in purveying his subject on the lecture platform as he is unflagging in the number of titles of his own publications. Forty-seven articles and books in ten years is the record of a great scholar; yet he is able to open his house once a week to the students in his classes, and not all comers can be admitted because of space limitations, and that in a large residence. We wish that there were more instances like this.

Students are quick to discern the anomaly of a teacher in a residential university who comes to the campus, meets his classes, and then retreats to hibernate until the next class. There is much wisdom in the statement which President William Allan Neilson once made to a young lady who was instructing at Smith and complained that the students took too much of her time outside of class: "Tea is the most significant thing that you can take while you are at Smith." Many will say that the judgment of students is not of particular concern other than its agency in maintaining morale. There is nevertheless an indictment in the inadequate motivation these time-clock punchers contribute to the student's development, for again we must insist that the intellectual and the social, the mental and the physical are not separable in the field of education. The professor has a responsibility toward student life, toward the development of the whole person, and this responsibility is met in class, in office, at the hockey rink, at fraternity functions. How can the maturity of undergradutes be enhanced when the professor fails to respond to an R.S.V.P. on an invitation to the Senior Prom? We view this as a failure of duty in the same terms as we view the year-in, year-out repetition of lecture notes read from the platform without any change of content, let alone qualification of that dog-eared reference to ten million at the bottom of one of the pages, be it dollars, years, or asses.

These, then, are some of the commitments of the faculty in the art of teaching At Brown the faculty is encouraged to participate also in the program of counseling and the response to this has been rich in dividends The freshmen are assigned in groups of ten to faculty members serving as advisers on a three-year rotational basis. The counselor clarifies, at the basic level, the philosophy of the curriculum. In many instances it is the counselor who can correct some of the false assumptions which entering students hold about the nature and goals of the liberal arts; both here and in the sciences where counseling is particularly necessary he can combat some of the glamorized notions freshmen have about the nature and function of science —space ships, huge salaries, and an easy life outside the laboratory. Because of the limitation of counselees to groups of ten, there is a greater impact from counseling on the whole faculty. The freshmen have more time to be counseled and the faculty member is more likely to come to know his charges, who they are, what they represent, and what ought to be done with them. A student is always more pliable in the presence of a teacher than before administrative officers. Deans can terrify students, and in their fear they seek refuge by piling their problems upon the registrar. Now the registrar is frequently one of the very few persons in the academic grove who is both systematic and possessed of understanding. Yet the wheels of the institution turn on the registrar, and the faculty is always waiting to see him; hence our belief that widespread counseling among the teaching staff is a desideratum. Presidents can bring out a good student response, but too frequently it is limited to social pleasantries. Often students do not recognize the stranger who accosts them on the campus and recognition has to be delayed until diplomas are awarded at the end of the senior year.

Professors, even the best of them, come in two varieties; there are those who are solicitous about the curriculum, its operation and all it entails, and those who flee like scared rabbits at even so much as mention of curricular details. Since the curriculum is perhaps the most important vehicle in the transmission of education, it should be of pertinent concern to all involved that its operation be effective, that it be constantly amended, tinkered with, revised, an object at once of some permanency and some experimentation, with the larger view of the tradition of liberal education and the immediate problems of the times. Academic counseling throughout faculty ranks is the most effective means of keeping a curriculum alive and fresh. The professor who does not engage in experiencing the curriculum through his counselees is the professor of vested interest, the chief retarding force in a modern university with the ostrich cry, "Back to the good old days!" How a teacher can yearn for these good old days and still be abreast of the barest implications of scholarship is a mystery. Counseling, therefore, is not only a must for the students, it is a necessity for the faculty, an obligation not alone in the art of teaching but even more pointedly for the welfare of the university. At Brown most of the ideas of implementing the curricula come not from a committee brooding well into the dinner hour over what to do next but from the teachers who have helped to revolutionize the concept of education, to vivify the best from the past in the workable realities of the present with a projection into the future. We venture to claim that, without counseling, a university will become stagnant, a performance of *Hamlet* without the Prince of Denmark.

We have mentioned administrative officers and it will be well to consider briefly the source of these stewards of a university's operation. The most effective administrators are those drawn from the ranks of the faculty. We say "most effective" rather than "most efficient," for the position of dean or of president is one essentially in human relations. Granted that such officials find themselves in roles far different from moderating and lending leadership to faculty and students, the immediate job at hand within the university demands the confidence of confreres and affinity with associates. A non-academic professional brought in from outside the institution may more readily surmount the battery of secretaries and records commonly associated with administrative procedure, but he speaks a language which is neither the students' nor the professors' and his thoughts and actions are those of the marketplace. His efficiency may be outstanding (this we certainly will be quick to grant), but we question whether the satisfactory completion of a job is the only compensation for undertaking an assignment. At Brown there are numerous opportunities for members of the faculty to participate in administrative affairs. Not only does this make for widening familiarity with the problems of an academic institution, it at once provides an investment of interest in the curriculum and a sense of responsibility in the very heart of education, namely the reconciliation of the practical with the theoretical. It insures a body of teachers who can assume positions of administration when these occur. It dispels much of the intolerance which may develop between faculty and administration. Above everything else, this *cursus decanorum* provides an association of responsibility with the other members of the faculty and, in particular, with all the undergraduates, a very essential ingredient in an institution which is at one with itself in function and in perspective.

A word is in place about academic visiting. With the intensive study of curricula since the war, institutions have become accustomed to squadrons of visitors who appear for a day or more to observe patterns of education in action. Foundations underwrite these visits and, indeed, several programs of lengthier duration such as the Carnegie Joint Internships in General Education and the Advancement of Teaching Internships under the Ford Foundation owe their origin and support to the farsighted concern of two of these foundations, at least, for development of teaching and administration. Possibly only those persons who have done their first teaching under one of these grants or who have observed curricula elsewhere can amply testify to the immense impact of these programs in the evolving picture of education and training in service.

It is our contention that leaves of absence whether granted as the result of private or public grant for research or teaching or in the rotational system common to most faculties for traveling or research are salutary for the morale and refreshment of the faculty. The incentive toward this which the Fulbright Act has realized has proven as tremendous in its inception among educators as in the expansiveness of research performed. Princeton has incorporated an especial stipulation for sabbaticals among its Bicentennial Preceptorships. Even if a professor teaches a term or a year at another institution, it is to the gain of all concerned—the teacher, his host institution, and the college he represents.

Nor can we disregard the value of simple, non-academic traveling.

An academician, as any professional person, is able to trace a vocational pattern in life around him and we attest that the chance to see the Roman wall in Northumberland is as valuable for the classicist as a visit to downtown Johannesburg for the sociologist or an opportunity to work in a laboratory in Wilmington for the chemist. This is a form of recreation with all the refreshment that recreation entails and the professor will return to his position with renewed energy and a new perspective toward the subject in hand. Sabbaticals and leaves of absence, therefore, should be granted with even greater frequency than their name implies. But the shortage of teachers and the desirability of maintaining some continuity of teaching program within a department combine to offset the free pursuit of this ideal. In this connection it is our feeling at Brown that academic progress can be hindered by two phenomena common to life. The first is the belief in the indispensable man and an exaggerated feeling that a whole program will collapse if this indispensable man is released for a sabbatical or to take another position. The second is the tenacity with which individuals come to cling to their own cherished field of activity. We grant that there is some reason for this tenacity in a field, an area, an author, or aspect of investigation. But too often the tenacity has very little correlation with the scholarly attributes of the field or subject. In the academic sphere these assume proportions which invite pressures, resistance, and all sorts of motivations which should be foreign to teaching and which are certainly hostile to scholarship. Quite unwittingly one man can sabotage the work of a whole department by his insistence upon giving his favorite course year in, year out, and his colleagues contribute little toward alleviating the situation, since they have been duped into regarding him as essential or indispensable. Recourse to the sabbatical can sometimes correct this false situation.

The institution of the sabbatical has been recognized in business and the appeal to universities and colleges in recent years to provide lecturers, humanistic or technical, for the stimulation of personnel is indicative of the esteem with which the term of re-creation is regarded in a field where pressures are perhaps as heavy as those in the collegiate. The thought of executives of a telephone company assembling at an institution of higher learning to hear lectures on Suerat, Voltaire, Beethoven, and Sophocles seems strange for personnel working in the field of technical mass communication. Yet the potential in the development of ideas and motivation toward creative imagination have more than repaid for the expenditure of time and money, as the directors of this program summarize it. We do not cite this for the purpose of drawing a precept for the academic profession, but we emphasize the point that the stimulation of ideas whether among undergraduates, faculty, or alumni is an investment whose dividends are indeed a certified risk.

The greater proportion of our thesis thus far has been concerned with the faculty in action, particularly with regard to the IC program. There is yet another aspect to the faculty. The IC program or any other curriculum is doomed unless this potentiality is developed and explored. We refer to the role and obligation of the faculty to seek out new ways of education. This section of our study might be termed "the faculty in contemplation," for, while it is through the curriculum committee that an experimental program is put into operation, it is the obligation of the whole faculty to see to it that the experiment does not end with implementation. A new curriculum represents blood in its conception, sweat in its mechanics, and tears in its operation. The fury of months of committee work, weasel words, and academic horse trading subsides in the belief that all will be well and serene once the recorder assigns students to sections and the great plan begins to move. But, at the very moment the curriculum goes into effect, it is the responsibility of the faculty to make its assessment of the prevailing operation in preparation for the next curriculum. Too often there is indifference and leisure while the curriculum goes unexamined and months pass with most of the student body passing through the loopholes of technicalities before the vigilance or enforcement committee of the faculty advances. What we are suggesting is not that the faculty serve as watchdogs; that is a minor function and can generally be relegated to the registrar and his cohorts or a committee on the curriculum. A committee on educational inquiry must be appointed, and this committee is pertinent as long as there is sensitivity to curricular matters in the faculty. Such a committee constitutes a body of trouble shooters and the committee itself functions regularly and makes recommendations of technicalities in the curriculum which might be considered for change.

The important and most imperative duty of the faculty beyond the line of teaching obligation is to maintain an atmosphere receptive to change, flux, refreshment. Without this spirit of inquest and change, the curriculum will settle like concrete, and all will be lost— all that has been fought for in previous months. We do not decry the role of tradition in a university, but we maintain that the best university is the university which is able to take up problems of curricula, problems of teaching, problems of examination of bodies of knowledge, to sift these in the light of changing standards, and to maintain a tradition that might be called "a liquid tradition" throughout the whole operation.   Conversely we are not revolutionaries in the belief that the university must be kept in a state of uproar.   There is, however, at Brown as at any other institution of its stature the necessity for the faculty to promote liberal education.   Our Charter specifies this in one of its few assertions about faculty obligation. There are stewards to keep the students fed and there are mentors to keep them physically coordinated, but in the "well ordering of this college" it is the faculty which must continue to exercise the initiative.

V   Experiment Into Action

"We shall swim the hard course, up the river, buffeted perhaps by the currents of public opinion, bumping the sensibilities of those who are taking the easy way of floating on their backs with the current, but we shall give the best that there is in education to those who can take it, all of them that we can provide for, but no more, for what we give cannot be spread thin, or it will lose its consistency."
— BARNABY C. KEENEY, PRESIDENT, BROWN UNIVERSITY

A prescribed curriculum is essentially a guide in education, not a law signifying conformity. It may be conceived of as a precept for choice, an instrument of suggestion, never as a canon of unqualified injunction. Through its curriculum an institution can at once suggest its educational goals, encouraging students to expatiate intellectually and through preference; it can advance and standardize those skills which are necessary for communication such as correct English usage, mathematical reckoning, and a control of foreign languages. Principally the virtue of a curriculum is derived from its effectiveness at displaying the various wares before the marketers and urging them to make comparisons and to select a pattern consistent with their interests and their aspirations. As we have already said, it is the major responsibility of the faculty to determine which wares should be made available.

Immediately after World War II the faculty at Brown University examined the objectives of an education in the liberal arts. It defined these, among other things, in two specific areas. An education in the liberal arts must first encourage the development of broad interests; it should provide the raw materials of attained knowledge and an appreciation of these in so far as they are pertinent to man's achievement in the humanities, in the sciences, and in the social studies. In the humanities the student would be exposed to the creative imagination of the ages with an end of cultivating a sense of taste and a dimension of values that can be perceived only through literature, philosophy, and the fine arts including music. Of science the objective is both creative and disciplinary, creative in that laboratories can instill habits of precision not commonly associated with other forms of learning, disciplinary as only the physical and biological sciences and mathematics will develop accuracy of thought. The

51

relation of man to his social environment, the sphere of the social sciences, is best demonstrated in history and economics and politics and sociology. Without this study of man in society there would be fostered a provincialism that would mock the humanities and the sciences.

The second area defined by the faculty was that of concentration. Concentration, or the field of the major, was specified as a goal in which the student would attain some "reasonable degree of mastery of some special field of intellectual interest." Defined as eight or more courses in a particular field, this requirement sought to inculcate a respect for an experience in an area of scholarship with or without an ultimate end of postgraduate training. There is implicit in this requirement the thesis that a college graduate in his profession or business will have the challenge of responsibility of thought and action the greater part of his life. To inure the student with some intensity in this major field, therefore, and to expose him to substantial accomplishment in the problems of advanced thought are two important goals of concentration.

In addition to these two objectives, the faculty specified proficiency in English and in one foreign language as auxiliary goals to be reached as soon as possible after matriculation. It is easy to label these requirements mere tools, and in a sense the ability to write clear and articulate English and to read and write a foreign language are nothing more than skills in communication. In a broader view, however, it was the opinion of the faculty that these specifications are the hallmarks of a liberal education; they constitute a tacit recognition that the student is capable of furthering his own education and developing his own urbanity, whether this be conceived of as selecting good literature or engaging in creative writing or even examining, at first hand, the logical precision of a Montaigne or of a Dante. We can discount conversational difficulties in the Gare de Lyon, as the Brunonian who is proficient in French endeavors to learn when the *Rome Express* will depart, let alone on what track, but we cannot overlook the perils Platonism presents in the Jowett translation.

Then there is the free elective. Provision for several of these was made in the curriculum. The thinking here has been that a student should be allowed a choice to follow up his own inclinations, matured as they would be after the prescribed courses. It is recognized that the best motivation for choice is not avocational or vocational interests, but academic incentive itself. Thus a student who has been fascinated in some area in philosophy may wish to return and take a course in ethics or again the presentation and approach of European history may mean the subsequent election of a course in medieval history or in the rise of liberalism. We do not have to mention a driving desire to take a course with this professor or with that teacher. The matter of the free elective we regard as a most integral part of the liberal education; to that end in the standard curriculum of 1946 the faculty at Brown has made every provision for electives, the number increasing as the student possesses the incentive to seek them. It can be shown that initiative is at work here as the student seeks to achieve his distribution credits as early as possible in order to undertake this subject or to hear that professor in a popular course.

Our immediate concern in this chapter, however, is not so much the philosophy and the nature of the curriculum as it is the first objective in the liberal arts, namely the courses which foster, in the freshman and sophomore years, the development of broad interests and supply the raw materials for the whole program. For the curriculum of 1946, the faculty voted a requirement of distribution courses divided among the three areas of humanities and social studies and biological-physical sciences. Superficially such an arrangement smacks of compromise. It cannot be denied that a faculty can be indifferent to curricular matters until a general revision of the course of study is proposed; then all leap to the defense of their own particular interests. The observation might be made that a curriculum is like a fireplug in a residential area: it can put out fires, but it is also an incentive for all the dogs in the neighborhood.

In operation, the curriculum of 1946 required students to pursue 12 distribution courses, four in each of the areas. Opportunity to meet the distribution requirements through reading and subsequent examination, what are called anticipatory tests, made for a certain flexibility in by-passing scheduling conflicts which might occur while increasing the number of free electives a student might pursue. While there were initial problems in getting students to perceive what it was all about and to arrange their own programs, this curriculum has stood as the standard curriculum for ten years. It is a tribute to the flexibility of this curriculum and to the broad educational philosophy which its framers incorporated that the 1958 curriculum at Brown which combines aspects of the standard and experimental curricula incorporates many of its specifications and most of its details of operation.

It has been a good curriculum in that it fulfills its aims and the ideals of the faculty. Behind it there was a great deal of thinking. Even today, an examination of its objectives, its goals, and its technique of presentation finds little that could have been added to improve it or to make it stronger as it was adopted. It has been a rich curriculum in that it has insured both breadth and depth. It has been a wise curriculum in that it has been no mere platter of survey courses, funeral meats served up from an earlier generation. The key word in this curriculum has been "distribution." In each of his 12 courses the student is given no broad sweeping generalization of trends and appreciation. The distribution course seeks to advance a body of information and, what is most important, to demonstrate the manner in which the scholarly mind discovers and examines and appraises this evidence.

For the student the distribution course represents a partnership in re-creative criticism; the student is shown the raw materials and the professor provides the plan for the finished product and its construction as well as a critical evaluation of both the materials and the result. In a sense, there is an element of participatory education here, for the student's responses are evoked critically as he considers the evidence and the aspect of the structure. Thus we observe that the distribution course in psychology not only presents some of the major facts and principles of human behavior; it also demonstrates, with the students often as the objects of the experiments, where data can be obtained for these facts and how these principles function in the media and atmosphere of society. A course in European history could well be a resumé of dates and events from the fall of Rome to the present day; our distribution course undertakes to emphasize the rise of liberalism as a determinant of and factor in the flow of time and the emergence of political and social consciousness in the institutions which have made for this.

By the very nature of this curriculum's stipulations, the lowerclassman is permitted to exercise choice in arranging his program. It is assured, however, that he will have two semesters of physical or biological science, two semesters of history, ancient or European, and at least one or two semesters of literature with philosophy or the history of the fine arts or the metaphysics of music. Expansion of choice to comprehend further work in science and the social studies is required. At this point the observation may be made that a totally prescribed curriculum, especially at this level, is very easy to administer. As the student's choice is broadened, administrative problems increase. Our curriculum has required much attention in the way of counseling; this we have given it willingly, for we believe that, over and above the pedagogical advantages which accrue from faculty advising, there is involved the vital concern of each student with education, his own and the institution's. It goes without saying that a student who is impressed with what the liberal arts signify is the best kind of alumnus we can send out into the world. Indifference to curricular matters may mean ultimate indifference to all forms of educational expression except what class will be seated on the 50-yard line twenty years after graduation.

The experimental curriculum of the Identification and Criticism of Ideas was initially superimposed upon our standard distribution curriculum. In planning for these new courses and their place in the curriculum, the administration and faculty were aware of certain problems that would arise. We considered the likelihood of a division in the student body with two groups pursuing separate courses of study; here there might be damage to the whole academic and social pattern; cleavage in the faculty also had to be considered. Availability of teaching staff presented still another difficulty, for, as we have said, which teacher would be willing to postpone his personal research to work up a course that was purely experimental, a kind of course that had never been given before, while his colleagues continued to broaden the boundaries of knowledge through research and accordingly advance in rank through publication? The desire of a department to participate in the program, moreover, was a factor. As with all curricula, it comes down to the individual teachers who must dictate its nature and who must possess the incentive to make it work. Collectively it is the department that must have the enthusiasm for experimental teaching. Again there was some sentiment that not all fields in our standard curriculum presented aspects that could be translated into the terms of the experimental courses.

To enhance the maneuverability of a curriculum containing two kinds of courses, it was recognized early in the first stages of planning that, since no student would be able to carry a program consisting solely of experimental courses (this because of the nature of the total curricular requirements at Brown) and furthermore because not all departments offered IC courses, the most immediate tasks were to designate which students would be admitted to the new courses and to limit the number of IC courses a student could include in his distribution requirement of 12 courses to be met by the end of the fifth semester. That is why the first stipulation was one of academic quality as reflected in the student's previous achievement in school or at Brown. Hence the initial requirement that, in the first year of operation, the IC courses could be elected by freshmen and sophomores who stood in the upper half of their class. For sophomores this standing was derived from work of the first year at college; attainments in the S.A.T. of the C.E.E.B. and class rank in secondary schools were the principal determinants among entering freshmen.

The limited enrollment ensured a fair and successful launching of the new program; in time the courses have been opened to any student who desires to take them. The second stipulation—limitation of the number of courses that can be included in a student's program—was more difficult to determine and to administer. Here are involved several factors. We believe that the nature of our standard distribution courses is important in the education of the student, and that each student should be exposed to this particular approach, at least in some of his courses. Again, not every department offers an IC course, while some departments present a whole battery of courses; this would prove to be a form of restraint in the free choice of distribution areas and fields. Finally, we took into consideration the expanding evolution of the new courses and, in the belief that no experiment admits full allegiance until the period of trial ends, we adopted an attitude of watchfulness and anticipation until we had evidence that the formulated courses were successful.

A student, accordingly, who had been admitted to the experimental program enriched his distribution pattern with IC courses. The pattern of courses pursued in freshman and sophomore years by all students in the standard curriculum, namely four courses in the sciences, four in the humanities, and four in the social sciences—for those students in the experimental curriculum this pattern was altered to permit the election of IC courses in each of the areas, sciences, humanities, and social studies, as few as three and as many as six in each area. Another regulation allowed each student to pursue at least two IC courses in the freshman year and at least two in the sophomore year. The remaining requirements of the curriculum could be fulfilled by four IC or standard courses. This has been the pattern since the first IC courses were introduced in 1953; new departmental offerings have been added; the number of departments presenting IC courses has increased; in these broad requirements, however, we have discovered the most effective procedure for administering the two curricula. The curriculum of 1958 specifies that a student shall obtain four distribution credits in each of the three areas: sciences and mathematics, humanities, and social studies. At least two and not more than eight credits of distribution shall be obtained in IC courses.

In this display of departmental offerings we attempt briefly to indicate the nature of the distribution courses which our lowerclassmen pursue in fulfillment of the curricula. With few exceptions (notably where a freshman or sophomore limits his distributive experience to IC courses alone through meeting more of the requirements in option by passing anticipatory tests on the material of standard courses) our undergraduates are exposed to the two representative techniques of presentation through choice. We do not consider Astronomy or Chemistry or Botany or Music for, while these departments offer standard courses for distribution credit, they have not projected any experimental courses. In juxtaposing the standard and experimental course within a department, we express our belief that the peculiar virtues of the two types become more meaningful as they are assessed within the interests and aims of each department. In one or two instances there is an element of romance as the impact of one type of course may be perceived upon the other. Finally, we feel that there is some virtue in accounting for the classics which our academic departments have chosen and in perceiving the ideals and goals which are realized from a study of the ideas therein. The packaging of many of these experimental courses is so attractive that we shall refer to them by their titles; a study yet is to be made upon the impact of an imaginative title on the lowerclassman as he makes his selection of courses. Some of these would qualify for a competition at Young and Rubicam in catching the public eye.

ART

The Department of Art seeks to interpret the history of man's achievement and his imagination through the study of the fine arts, painting, sculpture and architecture. While there is some work in the practical execution of the visual arts and instruction is given in the language of these arts, it is to the expression of "human history in the making" that the emphasis is directed in freshman and sophomore years.

The standard distribution course, Art D 1, has been most successful in its educational richness and in preparing for subsequent courses and their techniques of presentation. Not at all a survey of artistic masterpieces, Art D 1 undertakes to evaluate certain individual examples of visual art with the end of stimulating both its aesthetic and moral implications in the history of man. Here are united an incentive toward interpretation (this based on the creative aspects of civilization) and the development of taste.

The first IC course, entitled "The World of Art Today," sought to "consider the nature and growth of a selected group of current ideas about art" through exhaustive study of four separate areas of artistic expression. Thus, modern Impressionist Painting, the sculpture of the Athenian Parthenon, the sculpture of Chartres Cathedral, and the Renaissance sculpture of Michelangelo became the classical examples from which the students developed ideas moral and aesthetic and historical. One goal might be termed the artists' quest for reality and the pertinence of this defined reality to the different ages of man. The rich collection of modern Impressionist paintings in the Museum of the Rhode School of Design stimulated the association of student with masterpiece. As a project, students acquired a specialist's knowledge of at least one artist which was presented to the class in the form of a report. In many instances exercises in creative design—painting, drawing, sculpturing, and construction of stained glass models set forth some of the problems of the artist as he translated historical principles or emotions to his medium of expression. Music and literature were examined and appraised insofar as these reflected a trend of civilization captured also in the fine arts.

This course has continued since its inception with significant modifications in its emphasis upon ideas. The relation of form to content, the integrity of the artist as a human being and as a creator, the languages and media which the fine arts utilize have come in for varying appraisals and consideration. Some aspects of the original IC course have been projected into subsequent IC courses.

"The Language of Art" represents a quest into the problem "What is the language of Art, and what can it do?" with ideas originating principally from examples of modern art. Once analyzed the "language" is observed in its humanistic implications: art and time, art and place, and values in art. The close analysis of one artist's creative process, which has characterized the original course from the beginning, is the subject of "Freedom and Order in Art." Here is a study in tradition and design as they affect the artist and his expression; through the analysis of the life and works of a single artist (for which the facilities of the Rhode Island School of Design, the Boston Museum of Fine Arts are conveniently practical) the student seeks out and evaluates the ideas that are implied in both conformity and prerogative. "Image and Idea" gives practice in the discipline of "analyzing the image and identifying the idea." Here again extensive use of original works of painting and sculpture in the Rhode Island School of Design is yoked with the reading of a literary classic from

Greece, from the Middle Ages and from the 20th century with the end of analyzing the problems associated with "reading" the visual arts.

BIOLOGY

The study of animal life, its phenomenon and its structure constitutes the work of the Department of Biology. The introductory course, whether standard or experimental, is required for all subsequent work in the Department. At the undergraduate level the Department undertakes instructional responsibility for pre-medical requirements insofar as these involve comparative anatomy and embryology.

In a sense this Department is a pioneer in experimentation with its introductory courses. Considered as a science, the experimental course based upon Darwin's *Origin of Species* took its place among the first IC courses in the program. In the course of time, a series of original papers on the gene, in themselves classical landmarks in the study of biology, replaced Darwin as substance for the development of ideas. This Department also most recently has been the first to effect a combination of its standard course with the experimental. Whether this will point the way for other departments to consummate standard with experimental remains to be seen. What is significant, however, is that a field of science has taken the initiative in sparking an experimental course in science and, at that, in a subject which relies heavily on demonstrative laboratories. Of similar significance is the fact that a department which has commitments ranging from pre-medical preparation to governmental contracts for research in cancer is constantly reevaluating and appraising its lower-class offerings, maintaining that spirit of enlightened enquiry and realization of flux in the phenomena of men and institutions which has characterized the breed from Aristotle to J. Walter Wilson, chairman.

Until the standard and the experimental course were combined and a completely new dimension effected in the elementary course, Biology D 1, the standard course, was concerned with "the more important generalizations of biology and the phenomena upon which they are based such as the characteristics of all living things," their structure, nutrition, reproduction and integration. Lectures and laboratory demonstrations implemented the textbook.

The IC course based on Darwin was offered for two years. The modification came when experience showed that it was not the whole

Origin of Species but rather the central part of the classic, the theory of evolution, that possessed significance. This theory or the cell theory or the theory of the gene would serve admirably as the "big idea" for an experimental course. The theory of the gene was substituted for Darwin, and original papers from Mendel to Stadler and Sturtevant became the substance for ideas. Dr. Peters has pointed out that "the emphasis is not in genetics as an isolated biological discipline but rather on the relationship that knowledge concerning hereditary mechanisms has with all other biological knowledge."* Discussion among the whole class or in smaller groups pursuing independent projects (these later purveyed before the whole class) is supplemented by laboratory work in which the individual student plans and executes and then evaluates the material of the classic papers.

The new course, of two semester duration, has many of the aims of the D 1 and the IC courses. Lectures, discussions, directed and independent laboratories contribute to an exercise in "Experimental and Comparative Biology"—with the theory of the cell as the central theme of the first semester and organismic biology in the second. The same philosophy of change while maintaining standards for subsequent biological courses and participation in experimentation is representative of this new course. Such planning and such programming ensure that there is not a double standard, for here the professional and the neophyte are one.

CLASSICS

By tradition and interest the Department of Classics professes the history of classical antiquity. As a form of history, the study of Greece and Rome is properly within the area of the social studies. Proper evaluation of any ancient civilization, however, is dependent upon more than historical testimony. Language and literature, art and archaeology, philosophy and law are aspects of ancient civilization which serve to illuminate the historical appraisal of men and institutions. Thus, in addition to history and the social studies, the Classics may be characterized as a form of the humanities; in fact from the point of view of professional archaeology Classics can stand as a form of science.

In its offerings at Brown the Department of Classics presents courses both as humanities and as social studies. Classics D 1 - D 2

---

*See the appendix.

are appropriately entitled "Great Periods in Greek History" and "Great Periods in Roman History." Through lectures and readings designed to fulfill the qualification of depth in the standard curriculum, these courses are scheduled as social studies, and their essence is one of history as interpreted from historians, works of art, and masterpieces of literature. While these courses introduce the student to some of the problems of classical civilization interpreted from the historical and archaeological points of view, they have an additional relevance, in the fabric of the curriculum and of the Department, to all subsequent work in the field of the Classics at Brown.

In its function as a humanity, the Department offers Classics D 5 - D 6 also and this as literature. Ideally these courses should be presented in the original Latin and/or Greek. Because so few students enter college fully equipped to pursue quantities of literature in these languages, D 5 and D 6 have been designated as "courses in translation." D 5 seeks to satisfy the specifications of the standard curriculum as "Masterpieces in Roman Literature" alternating with "Human Destiny in Vergil's *Aeneid*." In "Masterpieces . . . ." several prominent Roman classics are read intensively with an end of spotlighting the nature of the Roman literary creative process; "Human Destiny" has an interesting history. Given first in 1954 as a standard course with lectures, it subsequently became a course in the experimental curriculum, first as a social study, then as a humanity, and now has resumed its original role as a standard distribution course. Classics D 6 is a standard course in "The Influence of the Classics upon English Literature;" it seeks to purvey some of the principles of comparative literature in the depth of distribution with the breadth necessitated by the very nature of the subject in related Greek and Roman and English literary classics.

As the central classic in the original IC course Aristotle's *Nicomachean Ethics* was chosen, and about it was designed a very popular course in "Humanism and Human Conduct." The novelty of Aristotle's *Ethics* as a subject for lowerclassmen in college is overshadowed by the immense wealth of ideas and pertinence to the ancient and modern scene which the *Ethics* displays. The relation of wisdom and virtue and problems of human conduct as they involve the social, ethical and political responsibility of man are central themes of this course; to this end it is scheduled as a social study. A variation in the central classic of this course is the substitution of Herodotus and Thucydides and Tacitus for Aristotle; the theme and the scheduling remain as before.

In addition to the IC course in Vergil which we have mentioned, the *Iliad* of Homer is the classic studied in another course "Reason and Emotion." The heroic concept of man is the idealized goal under investigation as well as problems of life and behavior as these occur in Humanities under Literature.

ECONOMICS

The structure of economic life constitutes the work of the Department of Economics. This form of social study, essentially a form of history insofar as money and markets are a causative factor of life, is ancient in concept. The rise of economic causation, however, as a motivating force in history did not loom large in the curriculum of the university until the 19th century. In all its developed ramifications and specialities, economics is extensive and impressive. The theory of value, the operation of currency as reflected in production and distribution of income, problems of labor and management, and statistics are some of the important aspects of Economics.

Economics D 1 in the standard curriculum seeks to present a sampling of these aspects with emphasis upon the philosophy and principles that have been derived from the past in their pertinence to the present and future. The emergence of housekeeping, the state, and international finance as determinants of economy are considered as principal factors in the analysis of the economic order. Because of the large amount of theory which this course involves, it is generally closed to freshmen: thus sophomores and upperclassmen will have attained more maturity in metaphysical thought when they elect this distribution course. The Department does well to avoid practical matters—how to earn a living, how to get a job with big business, how to become a successful salesman. Undergraduates have reported that it does enable them to read the stock market reports intelligently and that is virtuous.

The experimental courses are open to freshmen and sophomores, and of the three IC offerings each is concerned generally with one of the chief aspects of economy, however much each provides a sound basis for further work in the Department. The great name in modern Economics is of course Adam Smith. The *Wealth of Nations* is the classic enquiry into that area of history and philosophy which has been entitled Economic Liberalism. Consistent with the ideals of the experimental curriculum the original and continuing IC course "Political Economy" is directed to an analysis of Smith, his ideas, his pertinence and his significance in the face of other systems of economics. Other readings are derived from advocates of systems other than free enterprise, and in writers who have used Smith as a point of departure for further theories of free enterprise.

A second course "Economics and Public Policy" was introduced in 1955 with a more closely related association between the classic and the world of political reality. Keynes' *General Theory* and Marx' *Capital* are read and analyzed intensively along with Adam Smith for the economic ideas and their limitations and the impact which these classics have made upon society and the decisions of governments.

Pursuing further the wealth of potential ideas of Smith's classic, the Department of Economics projected an additional course in 1957, "The Intervention of Government in Economic Activity." To the *Wealth of Nations* have been added John Stuart Mill's *Political Economy* and Hawtrey's *Currency and Credit* as illustrative of the dominant and controlling ideas within another phase of economic thought.

Here, then, there is a resourcefulness in the reading and interpretation of the central classic, as the latter has affinity to several other significant documents which have become landmarks in the approach to economic analysis.

ENGLISH

The most extensive battery of IC courses in the curriculum is given by the Department of English. This department whose instructional responsibilities range from the training in the fundamentals of writing clear English prose for entering freshmen through courses in play production and a whole array of seminars in English and American literature for honors students has the largest instructional percentage of undergraduates at Brown. At the graduate level it is comparably lively.

Since the adoption of the standard curriculum in 1947, the Department of English has given a distribution course in literature with varying emphases and interests. But this two semester sequence has avoided admirably the tendency of such courses elsewhere; this course has never been a survey along chronological lines. If there is any shackle of conformity, it comes in arrangement of types. In conformity with the very essence of our concept of a distribution course, the two terms of literature are spent in a thorough analysis of a judicious selection of English and American classics. These

classics are changed from time to time as the fluidity of critical and
aesthetic interests change, but the novel and tragedy and comedy and
poetry are types generally represented, and the student is brought
to realize the meaning of literary expression and its implications. This
development of judgment and taste and reason we regard most highly,
and the aim of stimulating these attitudes in a course that stands
as a pre-requisite for subsequent concentration in the Department
is a happy and economical thought. That American literature plays
a significant role in courses in timely and encouraging.

From the outset of the experimental curriculum, the English Department has failed to recognize any one single volume or work as
a central Classic. Whether there is dissatisfaction about the King
James Version or a Shakespearean play or *Paradise Lost* or about 500
more English classics we are not permitted to say. The expansive
offerings of as many as 7 IC courses would seem to indicate that the
Department is more intent upon developing courses around an idea
or set of ideas than in allowing the students to derive their own ideas
from one author. The titles of these courses in themselves constitute
a course of delight to the planner of an experimental curriculum—
"Man's Faith and Fate," " Comedy and Laughter," "The Problem
of American Individualism," "The Voices of Poetry," "The Crisis of
Humanism in American," "Milton's Dramas of Struggle and Victory,"
"The Nature of Tragedy." But this effect of Madison Avenue does
not stop there, for the catalogue gives also some of the enticing
rhetorical questions the undergraduate tackles in these courses, e.g.
one course utilizes an impressive bibliography ranging from *Twelfth
Night* to Auden and Isherwood's *The Dog beneath the Skin* to bestir
freshmen and sophomores in answering "When do we laugh?" "Where
do we laugh?" "Why do we laugh?" Another course "Man's Faith
and Fate" running from Wordsworth's *Tintern Abbey* through T. S.
Eliot's *The Rock* stimulates students to see poetic answers to "What
is the nature of Man, What is the nature of Nature, What is the
nature of the Power that moves in Man and Nature? What is or
may be Man's Conduct or fate in relation to this Power?" Or again
in another course: "Who or what is a poet? What does he do, and
why? What should he do, and for whom? How does he do what
he does? Just how does his activity affect us? What does it do to us,
or make us do? What good is it? How can we tell?" The course in
"Milton's Dramas of Struggle and Victory" perhaps comes most
closely to fulfilling the original specification of the experiment in the
fact that *Paradise Lost, Paradise Regained*, and *Samson Agonistes*

are considered a trilogy wherein one author has expressed a unity of conviction through diverse media and situations. "The Problem of American Individualism," utilizing critically *Moby Dick* and *Walden* and Faulkner's *The Sound and the Fury* as the basis of ideas about a free individual in a free society, is a representative example of the Department's advancement of American literature.

We admire and applaud the enthusiasm which the Department of English has demonstrated in its cooperation with the experiment. Its failure to designate any one great English classic as worthy of a two-semester venture into ideas is amply compensated in its zeal to offer a group of courses of highly significant critical and stimulating presentation. If, as these courses demonstrate by their impact, a champion basketball player can become excited about T. S. Eliot's *Four Quartets* or, again, two hockey goalies are overheard arguing about the meaning of meaning in Coleridge's *Biographia Literaria,* then our students are richer for the experience. Also the question may be raised why two end men were attracted in the first place into a course on "The Voices of Poetry . . . Who or what is a poet? What does he do, and why? . . ."

GEOLOGY

Geology is a science which is concerned with the earth, its structure, its peculiarities, and its significance in the history of man. It is most scientific as it interprets and classifies the origin of geographical phenomena; it retains, however, a distinctly anthropological dimension in the fact that the life of man has been affected and shaped by land matter, climate, and the utilization of terrestrial resources. These two aspects of geology are emphasized in the standard courses at the lowerclass level.

"Physical Geology," which is an introductory course in the interpretation of geological evidence as the materials of land forms and structures demonstrate, is paired with "Historical Geology," an investigation into the historical aspects of the earth as it has affected life in North America. While each of these courses will satisfy one independent distribution unit in science in the standard curriculum, these two aspects of geology are combined in a third distribution course "Elementary Physical and Historical Geology" for which students must present a knowledge of chemistry. Not concerned merely with the origin and classification of geological phenomena, this course admits to a depth which we associate with the essence of distribution, and this depth is achieved through interpretation and the use of geological features for determining events and the pattern of events in geologic history. The student is not subjected to a display of rocks and topographic maps as ends in and by themselves; these rather signify the tools which the professional geologist uses as he undertakes a study of time and economics be it in mineralogy or paleontology or petrography.

In the academic year 1956-57 an IC course was introduced, and this course fulfills the experimental aspect of the curriculum. It is entitled "The Appalachians: A Key to Earth History." By fixing the Appalachians as the central "classic" of a course in ideas, Geology takes the honor away from Classics, for the date of the *Iliad* can certainly not be pushed back to a period of more than 3 figures B.C. The choice of the Appalachians we believe is a good one, though not that it is any better than the Alps or the Urals on geologic grounds. Students will however have a first hand opportunity to observe and experience some of the features of these mountains. There is moreover a considerable body of American scholarly data which may be consulted as the students affirm their own experience of evidence. Here geology and geography and biology and anthropology are concentrated and geologists aver that most of the phenomena and concepts of their science can be isolated and identified in this range within the University's own backyard. This then is an imaginative approach to the science of geology, consonant with the ideals of the experimental curriculum.

HISTORY

Among departments at Brown, History is in the unusual position of being called upon to revamp completely the notion of what lowerclassmen have come to believe the essence and purpose of history are. We say unusual because, while departments like the languages and literature can function on some assumed basis of maturity in the students' collegiate preparation, history can assume no such premise, for secondary students are taught or of themselves develop the belief that history is a chronological mass of dates and facts and events. Paul Revere's ride in 1775, the Norman Conquest of 1066, the fall of Rome in 530—these are indicative of the concept of history students possess. The wave of nationalism, struck up curiously after World War II by the *New York Times* for the study of more American history, has had some favorable impact upon the proper teaching of history in the senior year of secondary school, but the main issues of historical study are too frequently obfuscated by civics, social problems, political geography, and a plethora of well intentioned courses at school in the "art of understanding democracy at work."

With zest lowerclassmen leap into the distribution course at Brown entitled "European History since the Fall of Rome." By mid-semester there is considerable disillusionment about this course for the simple reason that it is well taught, its aims are high, and we value it as one of the most significant demonstrations of our philosophy of the distribution course in action. Eloquent and impressionable lectures drive the students to think for themselves about historical phenomena, betimes disperse some of the ideas commonly held of what history consists. The third meeting of the course each week is in the form of a class where the student and instructor discuss the implications of the reading and the student is forced to develop convictions and defend them. The nature of history demands some survey, but this is interpreted in form of trends rather than a futile memorization of notable events.

While a number of primary historical documents are used in the assignments in History D1 - D2, the experimental course, "The Growth of the Modern State," is constructed solely upon these primary historical sources from the thirteenth century to the present. In fact the comment has been made that no subject in the IC curriculum utilizes so fully so many volumes of the classics as this course. The concept of the state is analyzed from the high point of the medieval synthesis and the Renaissance to the modern state in an examination of Thomas of Aquinas' *Governance of Rulers*, Machiavelli's *The Prince* and More's *Utopia* through Marx' *Communist Manifesto* and Hitler's *Mein Kampf*. Representative documents demonstrative of the rise of political liberalism are Locke's *Social Contract*, Burke's *Reflections on the French Revolution*, Payne's *Rights of Man*, and Mill's *On Liberty* and *On Representative Government*. Among the several instructors in this course there is variation of emphasis as these classes go, e.g., one instructor used Edmund Wilson's *To the Finland Station* as supplementary to the readings in Lenin and Karpovich; another emphasizes Mussolini's *Fascism* as the most representative documentary expression of the totalitarian credo. The end of this course, however, is the perception into the rise of liberalism and its influence by and upon societies of men under the agreement of conscience and law. If primary documents give insight into historical causation, then this course is fulfilling a desperate need in the maturing aspect of the study of history.

MATHEMATICS

In developing its program of lowerclass instruction, the Department of Mathematics faces some of the same problems as the languages and English because of the uneven quality and quantity of the mathematics which students have had in secondary school. The traditional antidote for this lack of uniformity in breadth and dept is a battery of courses which will satisfy the needs of the students and will broaden the scope of mathematical thinking and practice for subsequent departmental work. Perspective and the professional excellence of this department at Brown have combined to obviate this fruitless expediency at the freshman-sophomore level. With the advent of the standard curriculum in 1946 the Department of Mathematics developed a distribution course in Mathematical Logic, and this course, an eminent example of the philosophy and ideals of the distributive concept, serves as a basis for all subsequent work in the Department. This course has been widely emulated and adopted at other institutions. Entitled "Fundamentals of Mathematics," Mathematics D 1 is described tersely as "an introduction to the logical structure which underlies mathematical procedures," but this is only a generalized statement. From the first grade to college, the student has been subjected to some form of mathematical symbolism, and it is a rare secondary school where the student is ever led to raise questions about what he is doing, what the mathematical concepts represent, and what reality the terms he employs possess. We might term this course an investigation into the phenomenon of number and logical processes, and in this respect its philosophical implications and aspects are striking. From the days that Plato projected the third section of his Divided Line to Susanne Langer's enthusiastic presentation of symbolism, this aspect of mathematics has been neglected, and we feel that this course not only fulfills the nature of the perfect distribution course as we conceive it but also is one of the most meaningful presentations of college mathematics in the modern curriculum.

The success of Math D 1 as well as the nature of its subject matter has raised doubts whether a successful IC course could be conceived. Planners of curricula and recorder's office lawyers have been skeptical whether mathematics could admit re-creative examination and scrutiny for ideas in the sense that these can be found in the sciences and humanities and social sciences. Short of scrutinizing mathematical functions for their practical application to commercial and scientific media, can the non-professional student of mathematics attain to any degree of competence in isolating ideas redolent of humanistic pertinence in a discipline which is in itself so completely symbolical?

The Department of Mathematics calls its IC course, "A Modern Introduction to Analytic Geometry and Calculus." This is essentially a course in the metaphysics of analytic geometry and calculus, and there are involved analyses of real numbers, sets, relations, and functions. Limits and continuity, differentiation, maxima and minima, superpositions and inverses—these are more than mere imposing functional epithets to fill out space in the University catalogue; these represent the essence of procedure and approach in mathematics, what in a standard course of analytic geometry and the calculus are mere assumptions. Through an examination of these assumptions and then the function of the proven assumption the rational of mathematical behavior and nature becomes meaningful for the thinker as well as for the potential scholar.

MODERN LANGUAGES

Custodians at Brown of a heritage which has given the world most of the major literary classics of Europe, the Division of Modern Languages is not concerned solely with the instruction of undergraduates in the languages of French, German, Italian, Spanish, and Russian. While its lowerclass patronage is directed chiefly toward achievement in a modern foreign language as a requirement of the curricula and in this respect a considerable proportion of the large teaching staff is concerned with instruction at pre-proficiency level, its distribution and IC courses serve as sound bases upon which all subsequent literary courses are predicated. Entrance into these basic courses, therefore, is contingent upon the attainment of language proficiency either when the student enters college or within his freshman year. These courses are indeed rich fare.

Among the standard distribution courses form comes in for emphasis—whether in French or Spanish or Italian or German, but it is form insofar as form is conditioned by philosophical content and to a lesser degree by subject matter. Literary trends and schools likewise are presented as expressions of national creative genius. In

French and Spanish and Italian and German a number of representative authors and periods are examined in these structural distribution courses.

From the outset of the experimental program, the Division has been active and it has not been content to create IC courses and then withhold appraisal and reexamination. In 1953 the IC course in French concentrated upon the "Ideas and Literary Problems in Voltaire's *Candide, Micromégas, Zadig,* and other works," and in addition to two sections where the basic texts were read in French one section was scheduled also in which Voltaire was read in English translation. More recently this course, still maintaining the goals of interest of the original course, has been broadened to include French classics from Voltaire to those of the twentieth century. All of the reading is done in French, and there is noticeable a trend toward emphasis upon those aspects of thought which the French classics have contributed to the making of the modern mind.

The original IC course in Spanish "The Interplay of the Novel and the Ideal in Don Quixote" has undergone something of a modification of status since its inception. Originally operated in two sections, one with the reading in Spanish, the other in English, this course explored "the countless perspectives . . . on human motives, values, and purposes" which this great novel contains. More recently this course has been reprojected as a standard distribution course, and while there are also representative readings from the Golden Age of Spanish literature to the present time, *Don Quixote* is emphasized throughout the year as "the outstanding expression of a fusion" of these two elements, the real and the ideal as spiritual factors in Spanish literature. For credit in literature this distribution course functions as an alternative to the standard course in Spanish literature.

The Italian and German and Russian sections of the Division of Modern Languages have never introduced experimental courses.

Of great promise, however, for the experimental ideal as well as for utilization of the wealth of European literary classics not otherwise utilized in language courses has been the emergence of two IC courses under the heading of "European Literature in Translation." "The Literary Treatment of the Emancipation of Women" derives its material from such diverse classics as Flaubert's *Madame Bovary,* Turgenev's *On the Eve,* Ibsen's *Doll's House,* and Strindberg's *Miss Julie.* The second course is entitled "Political Man." With Shakespeare's *Julius Caesar,* Stendhal's *The Red and the Black,* and Dostoyevski's *The Possessed* in its bibliography of classics, this course undertakes an examination of man's concern with political action and the reflection of the strong leader in literature and for life.

The nature and the popularity of these courses, even as is the case with the IC courses in Classics, indicate that literary ideas and values frequently transcend linguistic dimensions. They attest strongly to the impact of social and political influences upon literature and the possible phenomena of these conditions as a result of literary artists and schools. How much is lost in a translation, for instance, of Turgenev or of Buechner cannot concern us here. There is, however, ample evidence that students have undertaken further language study as a result of these courses in translation and we regard this as a fulfillment of one of the goals in the curriculum, standard or experimental.

PHILOSOPHY

An examination of courses in philosophy within the modern university will reveal that this subject is presented principally in courses of two types. In historical courses the thoughts and ideas of prominent philosophers from Plato to Lord Russell are displayed before the students along with some vague vocabulary of terminology and an indication of the philosophical areas in which these great thinkers have made contributions. Other courses, which we may term systematic for want of a better adjective, acquaint the students with some of the problems within a specified area like aesthetics, ethics, or metaphysics. In the latter there is some incentive for students to think for themselves, though in the light of his pre-collegiate training the average student will probably proceed to memorize theories of conduct, of fine arts, or of whatever he may be presented, be it Stoicism, pragmatism, existentialism, etc. In historical courses the natural urge to pinpoint each thinker or trend by a capsulized maxim is great; ask ten lowerclassmen what the Epicureans believed to be the goal of life, and the answer from nine of them will be "Eat, drink, and be merry for tomorrow we die"; the tenth may strike a little closer to home with "Eat, drink, and be merry as long as you don't have a hangover."

Our Department of Philosophy exercised uncanny perspicacity in this problem of presentational technique when it established the standard distribution course in 1946. Neither historical nor wholly systematic, these two semesters entitled "Philosophy and the Types of Human Experience" require from those who elect it full mental participation in a critical examination of the assumptions behind ethics, aesthetics, politics, science, religion and metaphysics. In evaluating these assumptions the student is forced to draw upon his own experience, and this with the fact that it is assumptions not facts that are being challenged demands the use of reasonable and critical faculties not normally associated with the conventional introductory course in philosophy. We do not have to add that this approach actualizes one of the principal premises in our philosophy of education that learning must begin within the student himself.

The experimental course remains essentially as it was introduced in 1953. It is a course revolving around two landmarks of philosophical expression, Plato's *Republic* and Locke's *Essay Concerning Human Understanding*. Occasionally Spinoza's *Ethics* has been substituted for Locke, but the ends of the course remain unchanged, to examine and to evaluate critically the problems of justice and knowledge as they are exhibited in Plato and Locke, to consider the aspects of ethics and politics, the criteria for knowledge, metaphysics and natural theology, and finally to develop in the student the ability to think logically and analytically upon any given topic. In the course of one year it is reported that virtually every problem raised by Plato and Locke had been examined critically—"individual and social morality, liberty, democracy, communism, the family, hedonism, cognition, infinity, free-will, substance, faith and reason, the existence of God," etc.*

Most exciting is the effect of this IC course when one professor comments that, while the members achieved no real unanimity on any single important problem, their beliefs were altered during the course of the year and those that were retained advanced from the "realm of dogma and prejudice to that of carefully thought-out conviction."* In conformity with our belief in change as a measured and restrained necessity in the educational world, we find this reaction refreshing, for we know that students are admirably prepared for scholarship or for life when they end their freshman or sophomore year with this ability to evaluate themselves and the world around them.

PHYSICS

Research commitments to government and industry, expert instruction at graduate and undergraduate level, an uncommon alert-

---

*See the appendix.

ness about the role of science in a liberal arts education, and an evangelistic circumspection about experimental courses for lower-classmen, these are the concerns of Brown's Department of Physics. Much has been written and considerably more has been spoken about the impossibility of purveying physical science in courses that will have both the depth for the potential scientist and the meaning-fulness for the non-scientist. We know of many institutions which have been groping their way for a "general education" course in the sciences, and we know of even more physicists who stoutly assert that the conventional approach to their subject is the only approach, viz. demonstrations and laboratories in the traditional areas of "nat-ural philosophy," general physics, heat, electricity, optics, sound, etc. In their perceptiveness of the place of physics among the liberal arts, we feel that our physicists have made a significant contribution not only to our lowerclass curriculum but more particularly to the teach-ing of science in contemporary institutions of higher learning.

The standard course, Elementary Physics, underwent complete revision and reorientation in 1951 with the end that physical con-cepts and laws, as traditionally conveyed, would have greater perti-nence and meaningfulness for contemporary aspects of the subject. Thus nuclear physics, its implications and its deviation from the elements of physics, is a significant part of this distribution course.

Though the Department did not cooperate in the first two years of the experimental curriculum, it has demonstrated by its two ex-perimental courses that it is vitally aware of the opportunities which are physical science's in the Identification and Criticism of Ideas. The first experimental course, "The Concept of Energy and Its In-fluence in the Life of Man," as taught by a professor of physics who is also the Dean of the Graduate School, is as its title indicates a course built around the central idea of Energy. Through selected readings from great scientists from the Pre-Socratic philosophers to the present day and through experiments which illuminate these writers' observations and conjectures the student is introduced to one of the transcending ideas in modern physics as well as in other sciences and in contemporary culture. This course has a vigor which is uncommon in elementary physics courses, and the imagination which conceived of such a topic in the first place maintains its rigor as the lowerclassmen are stimulated and challenged by an eminent physicist and educator.

A second course entitled "The Evolution of Atomic Physics" is concerned with the ideas that have made for the development of an important area of modern physics. The executive officer of the Department teaches this course, and students perform the five great experiments that are pertinent to atomic physics—the speed of light, the electrical charge of the electron, the mass of the electron, Planck's quantum constant, and the radiation spectrum of hydrogen. In this way students study and demonstrate for themselves the classic expression of modern physicists. Again, ingenuity in concept has made for a thorough and popular presentation of a timely subject.

We cannot wax too enthusiastic about the work of the physicists in this area. They have shown that physical science can meet the humanities and the social sciences on what has hitherto be construed as their own province. The physicists have amply demonstrated that they regard experimentation as vital in course-content as in laboratory technique. The response from students, also, is a factor which we cannot ignore; here is involved a popular appeal which undergraduates have not experienced in other courses in science.

POLITICAL SCIENCE

Political Science is a branch of history, history of the art of government studied in depth rather than in breadth. In this concentration upon the social contracts among men which have been called government, the focus is placed principally upon the metaphysical aspect of political institutions, their origin, their impact upon given periods of time, and their meaning for the present and future. Political theory, analyses of constitutions, and those phenomena which express the will of a leader or a small group upon a state such as totalitarianisms and absolutisms are areas in which the political scientist is at once a philosopher and a historian.

The principles of political science are presented at Brown in the standard distribution course. The student is challenged to analyze the prominent aspects of government—democracy, monarchy, communism, and fascism, constitutional interpretation, and the development of social recognition of the state. He does not range over the whole area of government from the primitive state to American democracy, but his training is in depth, and through interpretation of several significant institutions he acquires some bases for judgment in local, national, and international affairs.

It was natural, therefore, when the experimental courses were established, that political science would concentrate upon some of those classics that stand as monuments of political theory—Plato,

Aristotle, Cicero, Machiavelli, de Tocqueville, Locke, Lenin, et al. The original experimental course "The Political Ideal of Freedom" has remained virtually unchanged since it was first introduced. Attention is directed toward "three great themes: power, equality, and liberty." While there is collateral reading from many political formulators, Lord Acton's *Essays on Freedom and Power*, de Tocqueville's *Democracy in America* and *The Old Regime and the Revolution* remain as the standard classics in this course. The implications of this course are broad; there is a link between European governments and the experiment in representative democracy of the New World which led to the Declaration, the Constitution and the Bill of Rights; again in the pursuit of political theory the student is encouraged to analyze and criticize ideas rather than evaluate sheer historical data; finally the reading in de Tocqueville and Acton constitutes an area of significant thinking to which the student is unlikely elsewhere to be introduced, for in these theorists are contemporary reflections of the state of mind which introduced the concept of political change to Western thought.

More recently the Department of Political Science has enriched its contribution through a second IC course—"The Idea of World Peace." This is a study of the "origin, development, and the practice of the search for peace and security in the age of the nation-state such as the balance of power, arbitration, collective security, and international government." Readings range from Rousseau, Bentham, and Kant to the Charter of the United Nations. A useful volume of readings has been compiled for use in this course, though students are sometimes required to utilize a form of critical analysis which transcends even the experimental program and its demands; an odd page containing a personal letter from Cicero in exile to his beloved Tullia in its original Latin form, for some strange reason, was bound into the midst of a treatise on peace by an Italian statesman of the nineteenth century. The study of political peace is unusual, even though bibliography in this subject is extensive. Collegiate courses are generally limited to a consideration of "the Peace of—" and that's the end of it. Through the critical analysis of a number of meaningful classics and the psychological and political considerations which stimulated them, we feel that this course is as great a contribution to, as it is a significant departure from, the conventional manner of political thinking.

PSYCHOLOGY

At Brown psychology is a biological science. The exploration of human motivations and behavior is contingent upon the anatomical structure of man, and psychology is meaningful only when there is recognition that man's reflexes originate in his physical stature. The study of modern psychology has in it certain aspects of the humanities and social studies. Interpretation of the mind as a governor of human actions and the emphasis upon man's relation to and reaction amid society are facets of psychology which reveal themselves also in philosophy and in history. First and foremost, however, as our Department of Psychology states, psychology is objective like the other sciences, and its data arise from the observation of patterns of behavior and personality.

To this end the distribution course, D 1 "Elementary Psychology" undertakes through lectures, demonstrations, and laboratories to initiate the student into the major facts and principles of human behavior. This course has had a prerequisite of elementary biology, and in turn it is the course upon which all subsequent courses in psychology are predicated.

In the formulation of its initial experimental course, the Department has expressed some conviction that the standard course, while displaying a large number of facts which may be "forgotten or distorted" in a few years, may well become obsolete within the college years of an undergraduate. Experience within the Department showed that "not infrequently the senior student seemed rather ignorant of the contents of some background course taken several years before," so rapidly does the psychological picture change. In affording students in the IC courses the opportunity to "work through" some of the problems as the professional psychologist approaches them, through "reading, discussion, experimentation, writing, more reading, etc.," the Department expresses the optimistic sentiment that the student will be able not only to assess trends and ideas of the past (this is a fairly new and fast-changing science) but also "to read and evaluate the *dianetics* of tomorrow." *

"Psychology as the Science of Behavior," as the original experimental course was titled, begins with Pavlov's *Lectures on Conditioned Reflexes* and from it is traced the idea of behaviorism. This concept is further examined in Veller and Schoenfeld: *Principles of Psychology,*

---

* See the appendix.

Freud's *General Introduction to Psychoanalysis,* and Horney's *New Ways in Psychoanalysis.* Supplementary readings in classics are as diverse as William James' *Principles of Psychology,* Thorndike's *Animal Intelligence* and Darwin's *Descent of Man.* In the second semester the idea of Psychic Determinism is advanced from one of simple behaviorism as the students are exposed to the continuing wealth of learned papers by experimentalists like McDougall, Tolman, Hunter, Richter, and Liddell.

In 1955 a second experimental course, "Measurement of Mind," was introduced and here, with objective clarity, the techniques of investigation are displayed from original sources pertaining to sensation, intelligence, personality, and prejudice. Field trips for observation of techniques as they are practiced in mental hospitals are as integral a part of the demonstrations of some of these as are the investigation of IQ tests and record examinations.

It is both in its presentation of scientific material with an eye to the imaginative and the realities of life as well as in its reform of teaching methods for its field that we commend this Department, which, we must add, possesses also considerable kudos of a scholarly nature. We are anxious that this revitalization of teaching procedure will produce not only more thinkers who can analyze the patterns of behaviorism around them but also better professional psychologists for their metaphysic rather than their sheer accumulation of datable facts.

RELIGIOUS STUDIES

It was a prominent Rhode Islander, William Ellery Channing, who made the observation: "A book about which we cannot reason is of little worth. We profess to know of no book which demands the more frequent use of reason than the Bible." The Bible appropriately became the central classic in one of the original experimental courses at Brown—"Religious Ideas in the Bible." At that time this department was known as one of "Biblical Literature and the History of Religions," and its emphasis was directed toward the study of religious literature as a form of historical expression, with the historical and the aesthetic perhaps surpassing the philosophical and the essence of revelation. The experimental course was not wholly successful. Designed "to acquaint students at first hand with the principal religious ideas in the Bible" the course undertook too rich a fare for its

own ends. Establishment of the text and the whole relations of Jewish
and Christian ethical traditions constitute major problems in and
by themselves, and would merit years of study over and beyond
spelling out what a religious idea actually is.

Subsequent reorganizations of this field into the Department of
Religious Studies has brought a new experimental course: "God and
Destiny: The Bible and Western Man." This course augurs well
for the experimental program as it does for the new emphases of the
department. It seems to us that the introduction of "man" into the
consideration of the Bible makes for a more stable canon of reference
by which ideas may be explored and upon which the nature of revelation may be predicated. There is, moreover, in the consideration of
"Destiny" greater opportunity for theological and humanistic specula-
tion which we find desirable for young people to experience. The place
of the Bible in the Western Tradition, as its ideas make their impact
upon centuries of society, more than justifies the offering of this
course, and we regard this renewed experiment as a vital contribution
to the experimental curriculum. Here is a place for reason, here a
wealth of implication, and here an enlightened testimony of the measure of man as he is subject to a Force higher than himself. To identify that Force is one of the primary goals of all education.

The standard distribution course of the Department of Religious
Studies is considered a form of literature under the area of Humanities; the "History of Religions" makes " a sampling of the decisive
moments in the history of Judaism and Christianity" with "some
attention to primitive and Oriental materials for comparative purposes." Ample occasion is found in this course to analyze the impact
of religion and its literary masterpieces upon social and political life
and upon art.

SOCIOLOGY

The family, races and minority groups, collective behavior, and
population—these are a few of the social phenomena which the sociologist observes and analyzes. Our Department of Sociology therefore
is concerned with a broad area of social science dealing with groups
in society and the impact of these groups upon their members and
upon other groups. Through the scholarly orientation of several
members of the staff, problems in population and ecology occupy a
strong position in sociological evaluation. Nor can we overlook the
recent addition of cultural anthropology within the framework of the
Department, pertinently in relation to the American Indian.

It is gratifying to observe that the standard distribution course, "Social Groups and Social Change," emphasizes discussion rather heavily in its presentation. Herein are examined human groups and institutions as organisms that make for social change; religious organizations, political parties, pressure groups, the community and educational institutions are several of the more significant "arrangements" in which individuals concertedly bring about the ebb and flow of change. This course fulfills the aspect of distribution in the fact that the students are not only aroused to consider and "analyze some of the things going on around them" but also are shown how the professional sociologist evaluates what may seem obvious in life but what is a dynamic growth in life itself.

It was an English clergyman-academic who advanced the idea that the increase of population advances at a geometrical rate, while the increase of life moves on in an arithmetical ratio, and since the last few years of the 18th century there has been a great debate about this thesis of Thomas Malthus. Malthus' *Essay on the Principles of Population,* in a sense an antidote to the optimism of Rousseau and some of the excesses which the revolutionary air of the 18th century brought in its train, is a landmark in the field of Sociology. Even as Malthus' treatise grew out of an argument he had with his father, it has been a controversial document ever since. The experimental course in Sociology examines Malthus critically and it provides the basis for the consideration of "Man and Society." Society becomes "a population whose form and distribution have influenced the lives of individuals." Extension into other social theorists like Simmel provides further incentive to trace the meaningfulness of Malthus as man's relationship to man is predicated upon communication and various aspects of the social contract.

While this appraisal of content and subject matter of the distribution courses is a matter of historical record, we regard the very virtue of these courses to rest in their expression of the willingness of the several departments to experiment and adjust, to discover and to implement their individual interpretations of an outstanding philosophy of undergraduate education. Of significance also is the phenomenon where the subject of an experimental course is purveyed to a larger group in the form of a standard distribution course as has been the case in Spanish and Classics. The experiment in Biology with its attempt to combine the standard course with the features of the

IC course will be watched as one form of prognostication of a future experimental curriculum. Nor can we overlook the fact that the titles and the content of all of the courses testify to a vital concern on the part of the faculty to good teaching and enthusiastic presentation. Only in this way can we maintain that the "forming of the rising Generation" is an integral part of the University of the twentieth century.

VI Motivations and Incentives

"If the liberal arts college, the only institution except the Church which has a decisive role to play in the moral crisis of the world, restricts its responsibilities, these obligations will remain undischarged."
— HENRY MERRITT WRISTON, PRESIDENT EMERITUS, BROWN UNIVERSITY

Motivation, a critical attitude, a sense of taste, the ability to reflect —these are goals, ideals in the abstract, which months of planning and committee work and faculty meetings have sought to stimulate through the establishment of the experimental and standard curricula at Brown. Motivation, critical attitude, the cultivation of apprecia tion, and reflection—these are the principal ingredients which young men must acquire as they prepare to discharge the "Offices of Life." Motivation, a critical attitude, a sense of taste, and a fondness for reflection—these are making themselves evident on the campus of at least one University in the United States. We can never be concerned, however, as much with the impact of the curriculum and its immediate tangible expression as we are with the role of the liberal arts in the future of this country and the fulfillment of the American Dream.

Overcrowded conditions in the reading rooms of the Library, a soaring electric bill, the difficulty of locating a copy of the current *Times Literary Supplement*, the enormous sale of paperbacks in the University Store—these we could cite as evidence that for the students there is something in this matter of motivation. Campus politics, the endless argument between fraternities and independents, the all-night bull sessions, even dissatisfaction with a concert or recital all amply attest to a critical acumen among students when their own sensibilities are aroused and disturbed. We could comment at some length on the fact that the nature of man reveals itself in the number and character of Petty prints hung in dormitory rooms, while the Nature of Man will revel in those characters to be found within a Breughel scene or the mathematical exactitude which some artist down the hill has effected in a Klee-like pastel. To be impressed with the seriousness of life is out of character among young people of most generations; to impress one's character upon life is a novelty in education, but it is a tradition both ancient and honorable.

The Charter of Brown University has many quaint expressions of revolutionary freshness in it. Like a good many other institutions of Rhode Island and Providence Plantations, it excels in ambiguity, a peculiar kind of ambiguity in that it is at once broad and specific in its postulates for the operation of the College and the end of education, both democratic and orthodox. Many of the clauses hover in that rare mist of clericalism and liberalism; others favor both popular and discriminatingly perceptive education. "Respect for the Sciences" is a unique admonition in most colonial charters for institutions of higher learning; yet this original charter makes this specification in the same sentence with a provision that all religious controversies which arise shall occupy the attention of students and faculty alike, in essence the first pronouncement of the ideals of the Identification and Criticism of Ideas. There is, however, no phrase of this Charter which is at once so provocative and so meaningful for the eighteenth or any other century as the "preserving in the Community a Succession of Men duly qualified for Discharging the Offices of Life with usefulness and reputation."

The Charter is silent, almost auspiciously so, in qualifying the nature of these "Offices of Life," and it has been the quest of almost 200 years of higher education at Brown to determine the nature of and the prescription for meeting these "Offices." Here the appraisal must be in terms more relevant than either the acquisition of knowledge or the cultivation of systematic habits of study and thought. It is to be interpreted not alone in intellectual curiosity nor will it admit a solution in the stimulation of mutual respect between professor and student. The "Offices of Life" symbolize something more comprehensive and even more intangible than finding fragments of the great tradition and perceiving the order in which these may be pieced together.

The challenge of this Charter is essentially the challenge of the standard and experimental curricula. The purpose for "Discharging the Offices of Life" is the work of a curriculum and the University's atmosphere; yet to execute the "Offices of Life" is beyond the statutes of a faculty, a course announcement, or a diploma. It becomes rather a question of faith in the integrity of the graduate. Here the only contribution an institution can express is hope and good judgment.

A great many thoughtful Americans are troubled with the insinuating devices of modern advertising techniques. In the morning mail we discover that for ten cents we can have a "large handsomely bound volume which you will be glad to share with your friends—a magnificent volume containing four great novels condensed in readable form."

We turn on the radio and we are told that our musical instincts can be enhanced intellectually by acquiring a series of phonograph records containing snatches of "great music" ('why listen to a whole symphony when the composer has written his most treasured melody in one movement?'). What such appeals do not mention is the motivation on the part of the public to read the book in its original noncondensed form or listen to the whole symphony of which "this most treasured snatch" is an integral part. To arouse motivation and to create incentive that will become a part of man's nature we regard as one of the very significant aspects of education in preparation for the "Offices of Life." The Age of Apathy, manifested in such diverse areas as light voting, premature leaving of school, separation from college for "wider fields of usefulness," crash programs in science (feared by no one as much as the physical scientist)—this Age of Apathy can be traced to one source, failure of our educational processes and institutions to endow the student with some motivation. The "Offices of Life" imply more than keeping up with the Joneses, more than knowing what to do when caught unaware in a national crisis.

It is the business of undergraduate education to endow its students with a desire to educate themselves throughout their life, to walk in the great tradition which is the richer because a few thoughtful persons have had the initiative to act not upon impulse or upon the pattern alone of what has happened in the past. Rather they act through their own ability to perceive the problem and to actualize a prescription commensurate with the problem and with their familiarity with the "Offices of Life." To be enkindled with some enthusiasm for a subject is an experience which can come only to a student; a teacher can assist in this midwifery, but first and foremost it is the student who must have the incentive to carry on his own education. This we regard as the first prerequisite of education. On this obligation hang all responsibility and challenge. Given the proper motivation, the student will learn to seek out the "Offices of Life," face up to them, and discharge these dutifully. In this phase responsibility is important, the responsibility of institution and professor and student alike. To arouse this independence of thought and action we believe to be the most significant ingredient of a curriculum. The desperate need of American education is not more elaborate high schools and an augmented number of course offerings. Motivation can be found in the country high school where a mathematics teacher arouses her students to such a degree of enthusiasm that the class will be willing to stay after school once or twice a week to undertake the Calculus. It can come in college where a significant number of pre-medical students are majoring in Latin and Greek—the skillful surgeon needs more than technical proficiency as he performs an operation; he must also be armed with faith, the kind of faith that great literature and a study of social institutions can implant. Motivation can never be measured nor can it be purchased but it is the key to the "Offices of Life."

It would be naïve, however, for us to assume that motivation alone in our graduates is the only ingredient in the preparation for discharging the "Offices of Life." Self-interest and illiberality are natural concomitants of that incentive which projects itself in a cosmos lacking social awareness. To motivation and incentive therefore we must add the critical attitude. The graduate who has acquired the ability and willingness to discern the other side of the coin and other aspects and implications of a problem is perhaps in a stronger position socially to make judgments which are fair and to manifest an attitude of respect toward the opinions and sensibilities of other men. If, in every sentence our students hear from their professors or read in textbooks or central classics, they can perceive that there is an alternative way of thought and expression which may be closer to comprehensive truth, there is little likelihood that they will venture forth in the "Offices of Life" unprepared for what these have to offer. Professional and business life demands decisions that are incisive, yet reasonable, but they always involve the exercise of choice. The attributes of man's intellect are naturally endowed for this facileness; denial of this is certainly easy, and the history of past civilizations has shown the consequences of bias and indifference. Modern scientific contributions to relaxation and leisure assist in the uncritical approach to the problems of life and scholarship.

Man has a mind; he should employ it. Man has the power to reason; life itself discourages reason. It is our contention that undergraduate training extending as it does over a period of four years is an ideal champion of the cause of reason. In this process more is required than the sheer massing of data and accumulation of facts. We feel safe in saying that if every student approached every assignment critically there would be a revolution and it is doubtful if the American way of crash programs, critical shortages, and vacillating enthusiasm and lethargy would survive. Time, the emotions, commitment to the unessential, and a natural desire for leisure militate against the use of reason.

Great decisions, however, and advancement of the general state of knowledge are predicated upon the use of the mind as a weapon of challenge. The essence of advanced graduate training, notably the writing of a doctoral dissertation, should be the model for arousing a critical attitude in young people. But this form of education is professional, and we cannot expect to have students master this advanced technique of evaluating and sifting other men's contributions to knowledge in preparation for the bachelor's degree. An expeditious beginning, however, can be made in the years that students are with us. To arouse them to use their own minds, to instigate judgments upon valid evidence tempered by experience, and to forbid them to be content with what they find—these should be the goals of undergraduate instruction, if they will successfully discharge the "Offices of Life."

Glibly we speak about a meeting of minds. Eggheads and independents are rarely scrutinized for the key to their consciences. We express indignation when we read about the Americans who defected to the North Koreans, and we seek an explanation in some phrase like "brain-washing," and the clergy mount their pulpits to descry Pavlov and his trained dogs. Congressmen call for an examination of educational ideals, and the very educationalists who have done so much damage to our concept of liberal education serve up some platitudes seeking to divert the question from one of mentality to one of adjustment and personality. Yet it would be sensible to enquire what sort of academic training these defectors had in school or college. Were they fortified with some training in making decisions, in exercising a critical attitude in what was going on around them? Did they ever have a chance to acquire the facility of seeing the other side of the problems which confronted them before they were assigned to Korea? The mind is like a muscle; it is strengthened with use and with time.

The ability to examine critically what is set before the citizen must be at the heart of any useful educational system. Motivation and the critical attitude cannot be separated. Each complements the other. A critical attitude, however, is as much a moral virtue as it is an intellectual virtue. To spawn choices and then to exercise selection underscores initiative. It gives balance to life. It cushions hardship. It counsels awareness of others. It arouses recognition of these very "Offices of Life."

Then there is taste. Many will allege that this is an emotion or a facet of the senses. We nevertheless regard it also as an intellectual virtue, for it is capable of growth and development through the use of the mind. Its phenomenon commences with the early use of critical faculties. To paraphrase Cicero, taste is like the acquisition of the liberal arts: "it is the food of youth, the delight of old age, the ornament of prosperity, a place of refuge and comfort in times of adversity." Discrimination and evaluation are integral parts of consciousness; through these human nature can be nurtured and nourished. The projection of the individual into the world of sights and sounds around him brings full awareness of choice, and it is to the satisfaction of these choices that we cite taste and appreciation as formidable attributes of the educated man. The man who exercises his incentive and his critical faculties would soon find his spirit dehydrated were he not to possess the ability to rejuvenate his mind and emotions through an appraisal of art and music and literature. Taste enkindles the imagination; taste releas.. man from himself, at the same time stimulating revery and inspiration. It can relieve boredom and it can assuage tension. As we look around us and see the energetic pattern of student activities which a university community supplies, we regard it as a form of preparation for the "Offices of Life," as the student moves from the idealized citadel into the Utopia which he will have to create for himself. How much more relevant it is that the sense of appreciation which is instilled in the classroom depends and strengthens the conscience as the graduate ventures into the world and exercises the power to provide his own entertainment and amusement and enrichment. For more than one hundred years the older generation has been complaining of juvenile delinquency; this is no new complaint. A more valid criticism might be posed in the observation that young people have not cultivated a sense of taste and appreciation. Time hangs heavily on their hands because they have never been exposed to ideas or taught to utilize their minds or made aware of the rich implications in the conventional institutions and things around them. To channel their motivation in this area we regard the proper educational application as essential in preparation for the "Offices of Life."

Finally there is reflection. We are not counseling asceticism or solitude. But as the fever of life increases in intensity we advise resort to periods of thought and revery. This increases perspective, even as a sabbatical can promote scholarship and refreshment for a return to teaching. Unfortunately, though, few people have ever learned to think. Thought is frequently an exigency of the mind as a problem has to be solved. The faculty of thinking without an immediate problem at hand is difficult. Perhaps the most efficacious means to stimulate thought comes in the pursuit of the liberal arts. Here the scholar begins to perceive a nexus between sciences or disciplines. Here the college senior has impressed upon him what design pertains among the thirty-two diverse courses he has pursued over three or four years. Reflection is not limited to perceiving design among academic subjects. It is a necessity if one is to sense the meaning of life itself. A modern theologian has pronounced prayer to be nothing more than self-examination in a religious atmosphere and this has pertinence in the discharge of the "Offices of Life." Only those graduates who have the power and discipline to examine their motives and their actions can discern properly what these very "Offices" may imply. And so whether it consists of reflecting upon the intent of the artist or the motivation of men or the implications of a new gadget, the man who has been taught to handle abstract concepts, to recognize these and to evaluate them is in a more eminent position to adjudicate those decisions which are referred to him by his contemporaries or more pertinently the "Succession of Men . . . . in the Rising Generation." Distractions and amusements are calculated to take the place of thought and reflection, and these in themselves are of ephemeral significance. Taste alone can determine how wholesome and beneficial they may be to the spirit of man. But thought is ever available to the man who will engage in it, and this we regard as the greatest contribution an undergraduate curriculum can make. It demonstrates the strength of the will in its inception. It attests in its function to the character of the educated man.

APPENDIX

Six articles have appeared on individual departmental offerings in the experimental program. These will be of interest not only in the descriptions of the mechanics of the pertinent courses but more particularly in the departmental philosophy of education as this is implemented in the several courses.

Russell A. Peck and W. E. Haisley, Jr.: "A One-Semester Physics Course for Liberal Arts Students." *American Journal of Physics,* XXIII (1955) 440-449.

James A. Peters: "New Approach to Teaching Freshman Biology." *Bulletin* of the American Institute of Biological Sciences, VII (1957.) No. 3, 14-17.

Carl Pfaffmann and Harold Schlosberg: "The Identification and Criticism of Ideas: A New Approach to the Introductory Course in Psychology." *The American Psychologist,* XI (1956) 78-83.

Randall Stewart: "The Freshman Course Needs a Current of Ideas." *College English,* XVII (1955) 16-19.

Richard C. Taylor: "A New Approach to Teaching." *Journal of Higher Education,* XXVI (1955) 436-439.

John Rowe Workman: "Teaching Ideas in the *Aeneid." Classical Outlook,* XXXVI (1958) 1-3.